The Kitchen Witch's Guide
to Healing and Self-Care

The Kitchen Witch's Guide to Healing and Self-Care

Grounding and Nourishing Spells, Rituals, and Remedies

Maggie Haseman

ROCKRIDGE PRESS

To my mom, who helped me fall in love with cooking. And to my husband, who loves eating what I cook.

Copyright © 2022 by Rockridge Press

All rights reserved. No part of this publication may be reproduced, stored in a retrieval system, or transmitted in any form or by any means, electronic, mechanical, photocopying, recording, scanning, or otherwise without the prior written permission of the Publisher. Requests to the Publisher for permission should be addressed to the Permissions Department, Rockridge Press, 1955 Broadway, Suite 400, Oakland, CA 94612.

First Rockridge Press edition 2022

Rockridge Press and the Rockridge Press logo are trademarks or registered trademarks of Callisto Media Inc. and/or its affiliates in the United States and other countries and may not be used without written permission.

For general information on our other products and services, please contact our Customer Care Department within the United States at (866) 744-2665, or outside the United States at (510) 253-0500.

Hardcover ISBN: 979-8-88608-644-7
Paperback ISBN: 978-1-63878-443-2
eBook ISBN: 978-1-63878-694-8

Manufactured in the United States of America

Interior and Cover Designer: Jill Lee
Art Producer: Melissa Malinowsky
Editor: Chloe Moffett
Production Editor: Ellina Litmanovich
Production Manager: Holly Haydash

Illustrations © Mii Lab/Creative Market

10 9 8 7 6 5 4 3 2 1 0

CONTENTS

✦ Introduction ✦

Welcome, dear reader, as you begin along the path toward healing and self-care with the help of kitchen witchcraft. I hope you enjoy exploring this topic, and I'm delighted you have chosen me to guide you along the way.

As I found my path leading toward witchcraft about ten years ago, a natural branch of magic for me was that of the kitchen witch. You see, witchcraft is the practice of thinking, speaking, and acting with intention to take your life in the direction you desire. Anything can be sacred and magical when you put intention into it. This includes doing everyday things like cooking, cleaning, gardening, eating, self-care, and other daily activities. The heart of kitchen witchcraft is doing these with intention, which transforms a mundane chore into something magical and special.

I picked up on this from my mother. She genuinely enjoys the process of finding recipes, reading cookbooks, putting together the ingredients, and presenting the meal, all with love and care. She has a mystifying ability to look at the items in the refrigerator and pantry, select the exact right combination of ingredients, and present a delicious and nutritious meal. As she would say, it was something she "just whipped up." To me, it was like magic.

When I started expressing an interest in cooking, my grandmother encouraged me. For my birthday, she often gave me cooking gadgets and cookbooks. She taught home economics with the goal of ensuring that younger generations never lost the art of cooking, cleaning, and making things yourself. Every time I cook a meal or do house chores, I feel like I am honoring her memory.

Maintaining a welcoming, joyful energy in the space I share with my husband and our two cats is a form of self-care for me. I believe that a happy home makes for a happy life. For this reason, I wanted to focus on using kitchen witchcraft in the pursuit of healing through self-care in this book.

Self-care is the practice of taking actions in pursuit of healing all the areas of your life. This includes mental, physical, spiritual, and emotional health, as well as the relationships you have with others and with yourself, your creativity, and your ability to feel abundant.

This book is for you, whether you are a practicing witch of any path or are curious about claiming this label. You'll enjoy reading these pages whether you already relish domestic activities or are seeking guidance to help you love them. I think you'll also benefit from reading if you want support in practicing self-care for healing purposes. Inside you will find foundational information and the basic knowledge you'll need to approach kitchen witchcraft, healing, and self-care with confidence. The practical content will walk you through a variety of enchanting, engaging, and approachable spells, rituals, and recipes designed to help you heal yourself with the support of kitchen witchcraft.

Thank you for letting me share this journey with you. May the creations from your kitchen always be blessed. May those who gather there be filled with love and joy and peace.

✦ How to Use this Book ✦

This book is designed to help you better understand the methods involved in practicing kitchen witchcraft in conjunction with self-care and healing activities. Part 1 is where you will find foundational information about kitchen witchcraft, healing, and self-care, as well as the tools and materials you will use along the way. I recommend you read this through before going on to part 2, then referring back as needed.

Part 2 contains practical spells, remedies, and recipes for self-care that will help you apply what you've learned. Practice these as you shift your mindset into one of a kitchen witch. Pay attention to the ingredients and the procedure as you read through and create these meals and potions and conduct these rituals. Consider your own experience and whether the associations I share make sense to you or you would do something else. Then try that something else!

You don't necessarily need to go through and try these recipes, spells, and remedies in order, though you can if you want. You can also feel free to flip to any page based on the needs of your current circumstances and the area of your life that would benefit from healing.

Please remember that, as with anything else, it will take time to feel comfortable incorporating magic into your domestic life, especially if you are new to witchcraft and self-care. Over time, it will come more easily, and you will learn. The important thing is to follow your curiosity, experiment, observe the results, and enjoy the process.

PART I

An Introduction to Healing for a Kitchen Witch

In part 1 of this book, you'll learn everything you need to know about bringing magic into domestic activities through the practice of kitchen witchcraft. You'll also learn about healing through self-care and why kitchen witchcraft and self-care are ideal partners. You see, at its heart, magic is about being the best person you can be through seeking an equilibrium in all areas of your life: body, mind, and spirit. Magic is a practice of healing yourself and your loved ones and healing the earth and all the plants, animals, and rocks who share it with us. Recognizing that there is magic in the mundane is one of the easiest ways to present your favorite version of yourself to the world as you seek to make it better than you found it.

CHAPTER 1

THE MAGIC OF A KITCHEN WITCH

Are you ready to discover the magic in your kitchen? This chapter will be your guide as you explore the concept of kitchen witchery. The kitchen is a sacred space, and to a kitchen witch, the most basic household chore becomes an act of magic when it is done with intention. Cooking and eating have always been a vital fixture of human communities, and the kitchen similarly holds a central role in our lives. The practice of kitchen witchcraft is about transforming the energy of where you live, for yourself and those who live with you, as you take pride in your home and your family. Practicing kitchen witchcraft can also help you get in touch with nutrition and mindfulness and provide opportunities to try something new.

What Is a Kitchen Witch?

The main focus of a kitchen witch is to find sacredness and magic in everyday life and daily tasks and chores. For kitchen witches, that means cooking with magic and filling the home and garden with welcoming, joyful energy. To be a kitchen witch is to draw from the hallowed magic of the natural world as you go about your day and prepare brews, teas, elixirs, tinctures, powders, charm bags, and meals with intention.

Magical cooking is at the core of kitchen witchery, but it also includes household chores, such as cleaning, gardening, and maintaining finances, as well as practicing traditional arts and crafts like drying herbs, sewing, and soapmaking. Kitchen witches often prefer environmentally friendly and natural products for cleaning and hygiene. Additionally, kitchen witches tend to choose seasonal and local ingredients for spell work, divination, natural remedies, and cooking. Recycling, composting, and waste reduction are important to a kitchen witch, as is aligning with the cycles of nature.

What a Kitchen Witch Isn't

To be a kitchen witch, it's not necessary to spend all your time cooking elaborate meals in the kitchen. You also do not need to be a gourmet chef (though if you are, that's great, too). Kitchen witchcraft does not need to be flashy or complicated nor is it practiced solely in a kitchen.

Additionally, there is not a particular religion you must belong to; you can practice kitchen witchcraft regardless of your religious faith. While kitchen witches tend to be solitary practitioners, you are welcome to practice in a coven or another group. Finally, gender identity doesn't dictate who can or cannot practice kitchen witchcraft. Caring for your home and your family is a genderless act.

Alternative Names for a Kitchen Witch

A kitchen witch may be given other titles, such as cottage witch, hearth witch, or home witch. These names generally refer to the same type of witchcraft practice: one that is based around the tasks of running a home.

There are many types of witchcraft, and there's no need to limit yourself to just one title. Kitchen witchcraft can be part of your larger witchcraft practice or the only type of magic you engage in. The following are practices that may overlap with the realm of kitchen witchcraft.

Green, garden, or forest witchcraft: Deeply rooted in the energy of the natural world: the plants, animals, soils, rocks, weather, climate, and cosmic energy.

Hedge, astral, or spirit witchcraft: Based in spirit realm communication in which the witch crosses the boundary—or hedge—between the realms.

Traditional, old-world, or historical witchcraft: Looks to the "old ways" of the ancestors and folklore for guidance.

The Origins of Kitchen Witchcraft

Traditional societies have not historically separated life into boxes— home, work, family, friends, spirituality, health—the way many of us tend to do. For the most part, such societies do not recognize any barriers between the physical and spiritual: There is magic in every mundane action. It is from this belief that kitchen witchcraft emerged.

In the past, most humans lived closer to nature than many modern humans do now. Therefore, they needed to know more about the natural world: how to grow food, make tools, and heal ailments. Historical records show that villages often had a wise person whom others went to for guidance and healing. While stories of the wise people of the village are often romanticized, this was a person who intimately understood nature and used this wisdom to care for the bodies and spirits of the villagers, tell their fortunes, find lost things, and heal animals.

These wise people didn't have fancy tools and materials. They used what they had available to them: everyday objects like brooms, bottles, pitchforks, and candles and anything they could collect from the earth, such as stones, herbs, and bones. This is at the heart of kitchen witchcraft as well.

The Power of the Hearth

To early humans, fire was both something to fear and something to celebrate. It emerged suddenly, leaving death and destruction in its path, which was replaced with life-sustaining soil and new growth. After discovering the ability to create—and more important, control—the flames, early humans were not only able to navigate the dark night and keep warm, but it also unlocked a new way to eat, by transforming food through cooking it.

With the ability to cook, humans could consume new food sources and developed innovative tools for cooking. Cooking with fire alone leaves food charred in some places and raw in others. With the invention of the clay pot, food could be cooked evenly as the water in the pot absorbs the heat and disperses it uniformly throughout the food. The act of cooking slowly developed into a cultural experience where the pot contained the ingredients so the flavors could blend.

Then humans adapted their dwellings to accommodate an indoor fire. This central fire, or hearth, was usually placed at the center of the home or village where families could gather for warmth, storytelling, drying things out, and cooking and eating food.

The Central Role of the Kitchen in the Home

Have you ever noticed that people tend to congregate in the kitchen at parties? I remember very clearly how my grandmother found this both joyful and irksome. At holidays, parties, and family gatherings, she was always the head chef, giving jobs to anyone who made eye contact with her. Eventually, the whole party would be in the kitchen maneuvering around one another in an intricate dance. Then she'd shoo us all away only to start the process over again.

The kitchen is where the food comes from. People naturally gravitate to this area of the home to see what delicious concoction they can taste next. It is the center of the home, regardless of its physical proximity to the middle.

As a kitchen witch, the kitchen is central to your practice. As you'll see in chapter 4, everything you need for cooking magic into your food can be found within the kitchen. Whether you want to explore the world through cooking cultural dishes, experiment with the chemical reactions involved in baking, focus on simple meals the whole family enjoys, or turn on the kettle for an herbal brew, your kitchen will be the setting.

THE CONTEMPORARY KITCHEN WITCH

When you hear "kitchen witch," it may conjure images of a rural stone cottage with smoke rising from the chimney. Inside the cottage, a cauldron hangs over the dancing flames in a fireplace and a woman stirs the contents with a long wooden spoon. Herbs and vegetables from the garden outside and jars of dry ingredients adorn the walls. This image is quaint but is not an accurate picture of a contemporary kitchen witch.

In many parts of the world, the oven and stove top have replaced open fires, and people enjoy the luxuries of easy-to-manage cookware and utensils, plumbing that delivers drinking water into the home, and refrigeration that keeps food fresh and safe to eat.

As a contemporary kitchen witch, you can learn from your ancestors and evoke their aesthetic, while adapting their techniques to benefit from the conveniences of the modern world. For example, most of us do not grow or process all the ingredients we use, if any. We gather ingredients from places such as grocery stores, specialty food shops, farmers' markets, and co-ops. These options are convenient, saving time and, in some cases, money.

How the Kitchen Can Enhance Your Magic Work

Because the kitchen is the heart of the home, it is a wonderful place to do spell work. The kitchen is very conducive to magic as a place where something is created out of nothing when you blend and cook ingredients to transform them into meals.

Many people think about magic as something abstract or beyond our reach, but it doesn't have to be. Kitchen witchcraft reminds us that magic can be brought into even the most mundane of activities: the air we breathe, the water we drink, the food we eat. Throughout this book, you'll learn many ways to enhance your magic with kitchen witchcraft, but here are a few things to remember along the way.

Discover the Nourishing Power of Food

One of the most important things to remember about kitchen witchcraft is that it's all about connection. With modern conveniences, many of us have lost our connection to the origin of our food: the earth.

Food from the earth is one of the most basic and important elements of our lives, nourishing us, providing us with energy, and bringing us together. When you take the time to prepare and eat your food intentionally, you make a connection with food, with the earth, and with your own inner power.

To be a kitchen witch, it's not necessary to make everything "from scratch" and avoid processed and premade foods. However, it is important to be aware of the journey the food has gone through on its way to you. Kitchen witchcraft is an opportunity to reconnect to the earth and the nourishment it provides.

Provide Moments of Meditative Meal Preparation

When you cook or prepare food, it can be a wonderful opportunity to connect with the magic of the kitchen. This is especially true if you take the time to do it mindfully and meditatively. When you approach meal preparation with intention and focus, you infuse the food with magic. Later, when you eat this food, the magic begins its transformation within you.

One of the best ways to engage in meditative meal preparation is by using visualization. As you cook, take a moment to visualize your desired outcome. Visualization is, in some ways, a misnomer because it's not only about imagining the visual aspects of your desires. You'll also want to involve your other senses when imagining your desired reality. Consider the sounds, tastes, textures, emotions, smells, and images as you focus on what you want to be, do, or have.

Explore New Ingredients

There is a line that witches walk between the known and the unknown. Through scientific study, modern witches certainly know things that ancient people didn't, and we continue to explore the imagination, the spirit realm, and other mysteries.

Magic and witchcraft are about what you can do now in the physical realm to create the reality you want in the future. To get to the future reality that you desire, you have to be very conscious of your current reality, you have to be grounded in absolute and objective truth.

In kitchen witchcraft, you can satisfy this curiosity through exploring new ingredients, trying new flavors, and seeking out new recipes. This helps you expand your knowledge of cooking as you learn more about the magical properties of herbs and other ingredients and discover new ways to use them in spell work.

Embrace the Kitchen as a Sacred Space

The modern technologies in kitchen appliances and the invention of premade food make cooking faster and more convenient for the average person than it was one hundred years ago. It also sends a subliminal message that we should strive to limit our time in the kitchen.

The 1960s movement for gender equality pushed a narrative that a woman's place is not only in the kitchen and that her worth extends beyond the ability to run a household, which is true. At the same time, it perpetuated the idea that housework is inferior to work done outside of the home, which is not true.

A kitchen witch recognizes that the kitchen is a sacred space, and housework is spiritual work. To do this, you may need to examine your beliefs surrounding housework and other domestic tasks. It is common to consider these as chores you need to get done before you can move on to the better part of life. However, a kitchen witch revels in the sacredness of the kitchen and its symbolism as the hearth that connects us to our ancestors.

Whether you are new to kitchen witchcraft or have identified with the title for a long time, whether you enjoy cooking elaborate meals, are excited to experiment with fresh herbs and ingredients, or love making a warm mug of tea, you can embrace the kitchen as a sacred space for magic to happen.

Key Takeaways

In this chapter, you learned that no matter your level of experience with witchcraft or cooking and other domestic tasks, you can be a kitchen witch. When you create a meal, snack, or beverage in the heart of the home, you are creating something magical. Before you head into the next chapter about self-care and healing, absorb these key points.

✦ Kitchen witchcraft is not limited to cooking, but also includes other household tasks, such as cleaning, gardening, managing finances, and crafts.

✦ A kitchen witch can practice any religion or none, can practice alone or with a group, and can hold any identity (sexual orientation, gender expression, race, ethnicity, etc.).

✦ Kitchen witchcraft links humanity in a basic need across time and space from cooking over an open flame in a firepit to the modern fully equipped kitchen.

✦ The hearth is a sacred space, central to the home in daily life and as a gathering place for friends and family during holidays and parties.

✦ Bringing magic into the kitchen can enhance your life by nourishing your body, mind, and spirit, reminding you of mindfulness when preparing and eating food, and inviting you to explore new flavors.

CHAPTER 2

THE ROLE OF HEALING AND SELF-CARE

Self-care is important for everyone, including witches, but it can be challenging to find time for yourself on top of the other responsibilities you are juggling. It's important to remember that to show up for the things that matter to you, it is essential to take care of yourself. You can't pour from an empty cup, as they say.

In this chapter, you will learn about filling your cup through healing and self-care practices, including making your needs a priority, getting to know yourself, and approaching healing in a holistic manner. Consistent self-care can improve the various areas of your life: mind, body, spirit, and beyond. When it's a challenge, commit to your self-care practice by remembering that you are worthy of care.

What Is Healing?

The word "healing" comes from the Old English "hælan," which means "to make whole." Healing is a process of repairing a broken, injured, or damaged body part. The word can also refer to restoring your mental, spiritual, or emotional health, building your self-esteem, inspiring a creative spark, repairing a relationship, or unearthing abundance.

The healing process depends on your unique circumstances and needs, therefore there is no singular prescriptive method for healing. Sometimes you can heal on your own, other times you may need support from an external guide, such as a medical doctor, nutritionist, therapist, coach, teacher, trainer, or other professional.

Keep in mind that healing is a process. It begins after the initial harm is done, even if you aren't consciously aware of it. At some point, you may decide to intentionally commit to healing. As the process continues, you will need to check in to see where you are in comparison to when you started to ensure you are making progress.

What Is Self-Care?

The term "self-care" was coined in the 1950s and the concept spread during the 1960s civil rights activism, particularly among members of the Black Panther Party. Self-care for many marginalized communities at the time was the only form of care, due to systemic structures that limited access to basic health care. Additionally, activism requires incredible stamina, and many activists would burn out when they pushed themselves beyond their physical, mental, emotional, and spiritual limits. As Audre Lorde said in her book *A Burst of Light*, self-care is rooted in self-preservation, rather than self-indulgence.

From this history, self-care has emerged as a growing trend in holistic health care. It is the practice of taking care of yourself on every level. This means creating habits, rituals, and routines that benefit you physically, mentally, spiritually, and emotionally. It means committing to loving yourself and being compassionate toward yourself while being creative in the way you use your time, energy, and resources. Self-care also includes seeking out healthy relationships in which you feel supported and encouraged as you support and encourage your friends and family members.

When it comes to self-care, the goal is to learn how to recognize what you need in the various areas of your life and to honor these needs. Self-care is not about following every whim and desire. Doing things that bring you joy in the moment can be part of the overall self-care practice, but true self-care is about seeking long-term health and well-being.

The Benefits of Healing Through Self-Care

Self-care is a practice of promoting the process of healing. It's a compounding loop in which taking care of yourself promotes healing, and healing enables you to take care better of yourself. Take your time to discover a self-care and healing routine that works for you.

When you commit to healing through self-care, you may find improved physical, mental, and emotional health; increased happiness, productivity, creativity, and peace of mind; and decreased levels of stress, anxiety, and depression.

To reap the benefits of healing through self-care, you need to make yourself a priority, get to know yourself, and approach health and wellness holistically.

Make Yourself and Your Needs a Priority

A common stereotype surrounding self-care is that it is selfish, frivolous, and superficial. This is untrue. Claiming that self-care is selfish implies that the time you use to take care of yourself belongs to someone else, and when you claim it for yourself you let that person down. In reality, self-care is selfless because anything you do to fill your cup can then be shared with others. This is a much more meaningful way to approach how you feel about yourself and how you relate to others.

Committing to a regular self-care and healing routine means you need to learn how to prioritize your needs. You'll become more comfortable talking about your emotions and discover the value of feeling your best. You will learn to set boundaries around how and when you share your time, energy, and resources with others. When you make yourself and your needs a priority, you start to recognize that perfection is unattainable, and you learn to be more compassionate when acknowledging your imperfect beauty.

Get to Know Yourself on a Deeper Level

Another benefit of healing through self-care is that you get to know yourself on a deeper level. Self-knowledge is an ideal that humans have been striving to achieve for thousands of years. The ancient Greeks carved "Gnothi Seauton," which means "know thyself," in the walls at the Temple of Delphi. In *Poor Richard's Almanack*, Benjamin Franklin wrote, "There are three things extremely hard, steel, a diamond, and to know one's self."

Knowing yourself helps you take better care of yourself. Many people are out of touch with themselves and are unable to recognize their needs. As you make a conscious effort to care for your body, mind, spirit, and everything else, you will become better connected with the way these areas of your life indicate what you need.

Approach Health and Wellness Holistically

When you approach healing, it's helpful to look at the interconnectedness of the body, mind, and spirit, as well as other areas of your life. While self-healing is possible in some cases, it's important to seek health care from a variety of external sources as well. This means seeking out alternative therapies and healing techniques as well as Western medicine and pharmaceuticals. Many spiritual healers vilify drugs and medication, but taking prescription drugs and over-the-counter medicine does not make you any less spiritual.

Be careful to avoid blaming the victim when entering a world of healing through self-care. There is a commonly shared belief that medical problems begin in the mind and manifest as physical symptoms in the body, and that by maintaining a healthy lifestyle, with a good diet, exercise, and spiritual practice, you can stave off illness.

Magic is deeper than your intention and your thoughts. Magic requires you to be an active participant in your life. It helps you become aware of your opportunities, invites you to take action, opens your mind to new possibilities, shows you how to improve your performance, reminds you to rest and reflect, and supports you in releasing things that are harmful.

When you begin to believe that any health issue can be solved through thinking alone, you fall into a dangerous mindset. If your thoughts create your experience, then anything that happens to you—good or bad—is because of you. When you get sick or hurt, it's not your fault. Shaming yourself or someone else in this way can be psychologically damaging, which is counterproductive to healing all areas of your life.

Remember the goal of healing through self-care is to feel your best and to encourage long-term health and wellness. Your best may change from one day to the next, and that's okay. Take care of yourself at every level and be observant of how you change. Then apply care as you are able.

REFLECT ON YOUR OWN SELF-CARE

As I'm writing this chapter, I am visiting my family. My mother asks if I want to take a walk with her. I think, "No, I can't possibly take a minute away from writing," then pause as I realize the irony of neglecting my physical health and time with my family in favor of an hour of extra time to write about self-care. I close my laptop, stand up, and respond, "Sure! Let me put on real pants."

I can remember many points in my life that follow this same pattern. I have ADHD, and I tend to cycle through hyperfocusing on different dopamine-producing activities. As I've learned more about my neurodiversity, I am more aware of this pattern and can recognize when I am neglecting aspects of my personal care.

I invite you to become aware of your own patterns and either record them in a journal or sit in quiet contemplation. Think about how you feel when you need care and how you feel when you have been cared for. What signs indicate that you could take better care of yourself? What are some ways you can promote your long-term health and wellness?

Consistent Self-Care Can Improve Your Life in Many Ways

Now that you understand what self-care is and how it can benefit you, you may be wondering how to be consistent with self-care. A lot of people are under the impression that self-care is just one more thing they need to put on their to-do list and to later chastise themselves for not completing. The truth is that self-care can be simple and affordable, and it doesn't need to take a lot of time.

Once you've committed to taking better care of yourself, consistency is the easiest way to keep up with your needs. To be consistent, it helps to tack your self-care onto a habit you are already consistent with. This is called habit stacking. For example, if you wish to meditate daily, and you already brush your teeth each morning, you might meditate before or after brushing your teeth until meditation becomes a habit, too.

Your mind, body, and spirit all benefit from consistent self-care, as well as other areas of your life. Each area has specific needs and ideal approaches.

Mind

Caring for your mind is how you promote mental health. Mental health is a state of wellness that enables you to cope with the normal stresses of life, relate to others, and make choices that are in alignment with the life you want to live. Your mental health both affects and is affected by the other areas of your life.

Practice mental self-care by giving yourself time in calming silence with meditation or another reflection practice that works best for you, like journaling or reading the tarot. Spending time in silence is an opportunity to refresh your mind. The point is not to stop your thoughts, but to become mindful—or aware—of them. The more you practice this, the more you will be aware of your thoughts outside of silent reflection.

Body

Self-care for the body is about honoring the physical vessel for your consciousness and spirit. To do this, you need to develop a healthy relationship with your body by acknowledging the body you are in and thanking it for carrying you through the world.

Practice physical self-care by developing a positive relationship with food and drink and taking time to move your body in a way that feels loving and restorative. Because we all have different bodies, it's best to consult with a doctor or registered dietician for advice on what would benefit your body. Regardless of what your diet and exercise look like, physical self-care is about remembering that the food you eat is literally fuel, not only for your body, but also for your magic. Additionally, water is necessary for life, so make sure you are hydrated.

Spirit

Spirituality is the exploration of the human experience and the realization that all things are divine. I use this word to describe the interconnectivity of all life and matter through energy. In this way, divinity is not only an external force such as God, deities, the universe, spirit, an abstract concept, or something else. You are divine, your loved ones are as well, and the plants, animals, and rocks around you can also be seen as divine.

Therefore, taking care of yourself is a divine act of self-care. Additionally, building a relationship with the external divine energy— whatever that looks like to you—is self-care, too. Engage in worship, prayer, divination, and rituals or spell work that help you connect to divinity. You could also set up altars and shrines for your spiritual practice.

Difficult Emotions

Emotions are one of the easiest ways to connect with what your subconscious mind wants to communicate to your body and your conscious mind. Your subconscious mind triggers a physical sensation in your body that your conscious mind interprets as an emotional state.

Some emotions feel pleasant in the body, while others feel unpleasant and even painful. Practicing self-care for your emotional state is not about suppressing difficult emotions and only allowing yourself to feel emotions that are enjoyable. Emotional self-care is about learning how to process all emotions in a healthy way.

Practice emotional self-care by reflecting on the different areas of your life and your lens. Journaling is one practice that can help you do this. It is helpful for translating your thoughts into words that you can analyze and therefore understand your emotions better. Meditation or shadow work can also help with this.

Self-Love

Love comes in many forms, but it starts with you. When you fill your cup with love for yourself, it opens you up to receive love from others as well. This can result in more fulfilling, loving relationships with others because you are coming from a place of self-love, self-acceptance, and self-respect.

Encourage self-love by supporting yourself with encouraging thoughts and statements. Your mind believes what you tell it. Affirmations are statements you make to and about yourself as spoken or written words and are designed to influence the beliefs you have about yourself. Whenever you notice a mean thing you are thinking or saying about yourself, think or say something you love about yourself.

Energy and Creativity

Creativity is sparked when your personal energy is flowing through you. Sometimes the energy in your energy field can become stagnant or trapped, and one effective way to get it flowing again is to move your body. Movement activates your body and gets some blood flowing as you raise your heart rate, which can in turn spark your creativity.

To move your body, you do not need any special equipment, a gym membership, or instructions. Though if these are part of your joyful self-care practice, they are wonderful supports. No matter your movement capability, movement is cause for celebration. Allow this movement to fill you with joy as you realize what your body can do. You might also try something new. Getting out of your comfort zone can spark creativity.

Relationships

Relationships come in all shapes and sizes: parent and child, romantic, friendships, siblings, co-workers, and many more. Being in relationship with another person requires compromise and communication. There will be times when one person needs to take more, and the other person needs to give more. A healthy relationship will be balanced in the amount you give and the amount you take.

To maintain self-care in your relationships, it's important to set and uphold boundaries. Whether you give your time, energy, or resources, make sure you have what you need as well. By being selective with what you offer to others, you free yourself to do the things that are important to you or are in tune with your values. Setting boundaries is how you can give with one hand and replenish your well with the other.

Abundance and Prosperity

Another piece of self-care is inviting abundance and prosperity into your life. Many people associate abundance with money, but abundance can be a large quantity of anything. Therefore, abundance and prosperity is about recognizing where you feel rich.

I find the best way to feel abundant is to spend time in nature. The natural world, in its beauty, wildness, and abundant growth is one of the greatest gifts to us. If you live in a rural area, it may be easier to come across nature, but city-dwelling witches can find nature, too. You can be outside in a backyard or a shared outdoor space, or by visiting a city park, arboretum, or protected natural area. State and federal public lands are good places to find true wilderness.

Wherever you go, spend time observing the natural world. Watch the way the wind blows the leaves, find shapes in the clouds, follow an insect on its tiny journey, listen to the birds. The abundance of nature is a reminder that all of life is abundant.

Healing Yourself Begins with You

Having the knowledge about what self-care is and how you can heal the various areas of your life is only the first step. Now you need to make a commitment to take care of yourself. This is a choice you make in each moment. It's not always easy, but it is possible.

In part 2 of this book, you will find several helpful tools, rituals, practices, and spells for using kitchen witchcraft to help you on your self-care journey. It's up to you to use these in order to care for yourself.

At the same time, it is truly uplifting to find support in the form of a community, whether that is a coven or spiritual group, your family, or your friends. A community is a space where you can share your challenges without judgment, and where you will receive love and kindness in return. Additionally, community gives you a new lens through which to look at yourself and shows you that you are worthy of the love you are receiving. You can see the way other people take care of you, which is an amazing first step toward learning how to take care of yourself. When you see yourself through someone else's eyes, it's hard to be mean to yourself.

Key Takeaways

When you look at the essence of self-care, it is about self-respect. Through self-care, you are making a declaration that you are important and worthy. It is about committing to feeling the best you can each day as you reconnect with yourself, make yourself a priority, live in the moment, and honor your mental, physical, spiritual, and emotional needs. Take these key points with you as you move into chapter 3.

✦ Healing is a process of repairing a body part, restoring your mental, spiritual, or emotional health, building your self-esteem, inspiring the creative spark, repairing a relationship, or discovering abundance.

✦ The goal of self-care is to learn how to recognize what you need for long-term health and wellness in the various areas of your life and to honor those needs.

✦ There are many benefits of healing yourself through self-care, including learning how to make your needs a priority, getting to know yourself, and approaching health holistically.

✦ Consistent self-care can improve your life in many areas: mind, body, spirit, emotions, love, creativity, relationships, and abundance.

✦ While it's up to you to take care of yourself, a community can be there to support you in this pursuit.

CHAPTER 3

ENHANCE YOUR HEALING AND SELF-CARE WITH KITCHEN WITCHCRAFT

A recent comment on one of my Instagram posts sums up how you can enhance your healing and self-care practice with witchcraft. It said, "Witchcraft is mostly doing the homework my therapist gives me but with better incense, candles, and baths."

Equipped with your knowledge of kitchen witchcraft and healing with self-care, it's time to discover how you can combine them. In this chapter, you will learn about the witch archetype and how you can practice witchcraft today while maintaining the healing and care that have always been at the heart of witchcraft. Later, you'll discover how kitchen witchcraft supports self-care through nourishment, mindfulness, and creativity. Then you'll find a section on emphasizing self-care in your craft through being open-minded, setting intentions, feeling good, creating habits, and recording your progress.

How You Can Heal through Witchcraft Today

Something I love about humans is that our evolution was propelled not due to our genius, but due to our ability to teach each other and learn things socially. It is through this uniquely human characteristic that our collective knowledge is passed from one generation to the next. This includes the practice of witchcraft and using magic. Witchcraft is the original healing and self-care practice.

In some ways, the methods we use in witchcraft are effective because they are echoed by many people across time and space. The first time a person does something or uses something for a specific purpose, it is intuitive. This method or tool is communicated to other witches and when that spell, ritual, or recipe is repeated or when that ingredient or tool is reused in that way, it gains power. By passing magical lore from one witch to the next, the knowledge of the method or tool spreads and strengthens.

In this book, you will find spells, rituals, and recipes for taking care of yourself as you pursue healing. They are created and adapted using information that has been shared by those who came before us. With that said, I want you to feel empowered to trust your own intuition about the procedure and ingredients. If you don't feel a connection to a procedure, a particular way to use an ingredient, or something else, it's okay to change things.

The Healing Powers of the Kitchen

Whether you are a practicing kitchen witch or not, making food for yourself and for others is inherently magical. There is magic woven into passing plates around a dining table, laughing with the people you care about, and sharing a meal.

Through practicing kitchen witchcraft and doing domestic tasks with focused intention, you enhance this inherent magic. Being intentional in the kitchen about healing yourself through self-care combines the magical transformation of cooking and digesting food with the magical intention of your desire.

Magic works through a transformation process that begins in the mind. When you focus on a single thought or emotion, it is sent into the spiritual realm, a place that cannot be experienced with physical senses, where immaterial things exist. Then you begin to perceive the changes and opportunities that are in alignment with that intention with your physical senses. You can act in the physical realm toward making that intention a reality, and it will eventually manifest.

How Do Kitchen Witch Rituals Support Self-Care?

The longer I practice witchcraft, the more I find that simple magic found in mundane moments of the day is just as powerful as elaborate rituals, if not more. For this reason, kitchen witchcraft and incorporating magic into domestic work supports self-care beautifully.

On those days when we become overwhelmed with the things that need to be done, many of us let our spiritual practice slide to the bottom of the to-do list. You may know that connecting inward will improve your mood, ease the pressure, and help you face challenges head-on. Even with this knowledge, it's easier to justify spending your time and energy on basic needs like eating, sleeping, cleaning, and earning money to pay for these things.

By incorporating magic into these seemingly mundane tasks and finding the magic they inherently possess, you can easily balance your responsibilities and basic needs with your desires and spiritual fulfillment. Taking care of yourself, your home, and your loved ones becomes the ritual.

There are a few things to keep in mind when it comes to supporting your self-care practice with kitchen witchcraft: choosing ingredients that nourish you on every level, slowing down to enjoy the cooking process, and being creative with your domestic activities.

Nourish Yourself with Powerful Foods

What makes a food nourishing will depend on what you need for your physical health. But food can also be nourishing for your mental, emotional, and spiritual health. Some foods may make you feel more connected to another person and can nourish the relationship, and some foods can help you love yourself more. The point is nourishment is not solely about the nutrient density of the food, and it's not the same for each person.

As you practice kitchen witchcraft, treat your food like an experiment. By that, I mean pay attention to how it makes you feel to prepare, cook, and eat the food. Consider how that ingredient or meal enhances or diminishes your enjoyment in various areas of your life.

Take Time to Slow Down and Connect

Kitchen witchcraft is about putting your personal energy into all the domestic tasks you engage in. This means that the more you do yourself, the more magic you put into it. For example, slice your vegetables, make soup stock, grow herbs and vegetables, and so on. Not only will you put more of your energy into these actions, but you will also feel more connected to the food you are eating.

There's no need to make things complicated, especially if it feels like a chore or you feel too busy. Slowing down and connecting with what you're doing can be as simple as painting a sigil on your toast with jam, splashing moon water into your cooking pot, or adding a dash of an herb that aligns with your intention at the end of the cooking process. Whether you are relaxed or completely frazzled, you can benefit from this moment of mindfulness.

Invite Creativity into Your Home and Meals

There are many magical paths to follow. One way to differentiate these paths is to make a distinction between ceremonial magic and folk magic. Ceremonial magic relies on precise, complicated rituals and intricate correspondences, as dictated by the book. This branch of magic is largely spiritual, with the purpose of gaining divine knowledge and discovering one's purpose.

Contrasting this is folk magic, which includes kitchen witchcraft. Folk magic is based in the physical realm. The rituals associated with folk magic are not rigidly set by a book but are created intuitively, using tools and materials the practitioner has freely available: keys, rocks, coins, food items, etc. As you engage in kitchen witchcraft practices to enhance your self-care and healing journey, you'll want to be creative with the resources you have and intuitively determine how they can be used.

How to Emphasize Self-Care in Your Craft

Self-care is about self-respect and making the declaration to the world and to yourself that you are important and worthy of care. It's crucial to your magical practice because your power is rooted in your ability to claim it. No matter what your witchcraft practice looks like, you can emphasize self-care. Integrate magic into your self-care practice and self-care into your witchcraft practice with the help of your intuition.

The more physically, emotionally, and spiritually healthy you are, the more you have to offer the world. To make self-care a priority, start by being open-minded when it comes to new ideas. You'll also want to set the intention that you want to care for yourself and promote healing. Tune in to your emotional state, and do the things that make you feel good, then establish the habit of taking care of yourself on a regular basis. Throughout the process, keep a grimoire or journal of the progress and what you are experiencing.

Stay Open to New Spells, Rituals, and Remedies

Opening yourself up to new things may seem simple, but it can also lead you to confusion, especially if new information conflicts with what you previously held true. It is necessary to be open-minded when it comes to practicing witchcraft because it helps you be a more critical thinker.

To be open-minded is to be willing to consider other perspectives and try out new things. If you become very dogmatic in the way you practice, it can keep you from the cycle of reflection and growth that allows you to remain healthy. To be open also means you ask questions and seek out information that challenges your beliefs. Whenever you are presented with something, ask why the procedure is presented in the order it is and why certain ingredients were chosen. This will help you understand more about the magical method and show you how you can adjust a spell to suit your resources, beliefs, and abilities.

Make Your Intentions Known

An intention is a descriptive statement about what you want or your desired outcome. You can set intentions for any activity you engage in, including spells, domestic tasks, work projects, self-care, and relationships. Whatever the activity, think, speak, or write an intention for it. Focus on that intention with clarity and without distraction. Then take action that is in alignment with that intention.

The more specific and precise you can be about your intention, the better. Consider what you are trying to accomplish, when you want it to happen, why you want it, how it can change your life, how it will make you feel, and who else it might affect. For example, if you want to heal a broken heart, think about how it feels to have a whole heart, what you'll be capable of doing when you're no longer grieving, and who you could meet when you are ready to trust someone with your heart again.

It can also be helpful to use "I" statements when speaking about your desires. The reason using words like, "I," "me," or "my" is powerful is because your conscious mind and subconscious mind both perk up when you talk about yourself. When you say things about yourself in the first person, your mind believes it to be true.

Do What Makes You Feel Good

Taking care of yourself requires being in touch with your emotions and how you feel. This takes practice, especially if you are not in tune with how your emotions feel in your body and the sensations they create. However, once you are aware of the emotions that are pleasant experiences, you can do more things that feel good. Take four or five moments each day to check in with yourself. Describe the way your body feels, the physical sensations, emotions, temperature, pressure, or anything else that you notice.

Observe what you are doing as well. If what you are doing is creating pleasant emotions, remember this and look for more opportunities to do this again. If what you are doing is creating unpleasant sensations, reflect on why that is and if there is a way to make it more enjoyable or give it to someone else to do.

Make a Habit of Regular Self-Care

A habit is something you do automatically without even thinking. For example, you might automatically lock the door when you get home or make a pot of tea every morning. These habits are learned, and you can teach yourself to develop any habit you want. Practice a habit enough, and it will feel as natural to you as brushing your teeth in the morning.

Here's a caution: When you get busy or stressed out, your new magical self-care habits will likely be the first thing you forget. Creating a visual tracker for your habits can be helpful. Try placing stickers on a monthly calendar, making a grid and coloring in the squares, or moving crystals from one bowl to another every day you practice self-care at least once. When you do this, it reminds you of your commitment to that habit. It also shows you what you've done and what you have the potential to do still, so that if you miss a day, you are less likely to give up.

Keep a Grimoire or Journal

A grimoire is a personalized book that contains any kind of magical information. It is a collection of the tales, myths, spells, correspondences, and ideas that resonate with you, as well as your personal writing and drawing. A grimoire is as unique as the witch who created it and includes only what is integral to their practice.

For a kitchen witch, a grimoire may resemble a cookbook. While a cookbook generally contains strictly culinary information and recipes, your grimoire might also include magical information about food, ingredients, timing, correspondences, tools, and any other information that is relevant to your witchcraft practice and self-care journey.

Regardless of what the grimoire looks like or contains, it is special. It's important for you to create a grimoire that is specific to your needs as a witch, your lifestyle, and your magical practice.

BE CAREFUL HOW YOU USE KITCHEN MAGIC

Remember to focus your intention and your magic on your own thoughts, words, and actions because these are truly the only things you have control over. You can decide what you believe and how you react to external stimuli. On that note, you do not have any control over someone else. It's a waste of your time and energy to try to influence someone else, regardless of whether you intend to help them or harm them. Their beliefs and thoughts can influence your magic in unexpected ways.

If the person you are doing magic on is in a good place physically, emotionally, and mentally, the spell will have different results than if they are vulnerable. If they don't believe in magic or they have limiting beliefs surrounding the theme of the spell, this will also influence how it affects them.

It's best to simply focus on the changes you wish to see in your life. For example, if you are looking for a partner for business or romance, be sure to think of the qualities you would want in a person to fill that role in your life rather than a specific person.

Your Spell Work Reflects Your Energy

When you practice witchcraft, consider what you are bringing to the table—or the kitchen table. This means that what you are thinking, feeling, and saying, and the way you are moving, will be reflected in the magic.

For example, if you are doing a spell to heal yourself in some way, instead of focusing on how sick or broken you feel, think of how it feels to be healthy and what you are capable of when you are most vital. If you are seeking a new job, don't think about how annoying your boss is and the awful traffic on your commute. Focus on what it would be like to feel fulfilled and purposeful in your chosen profession.

As you are cleaning your kitchen, preparing the ingredients, cooking the flavors together, and sitting down to enjoy your creation, keep your intention in mind. Don't bang cupboard doors angrily, rush the process, or toss things carelessly. Be very intentional with your thoughts and actions. You are literally what you eat and, therefore, you want to put the energy you want to become into the food you make.

Key Takeaways

In this chapter, you learned how to enrich your healing and self-care with kitchen witchcraft by learning about the roots of witchcraft, which grew out of healing practices. The essential practice of taking care of your energy and your emotional, physical, mental, and spiritual health can be enhanced by magic. In the next chapter, you will find practical information about the tangible and intangible tools and materials of a kitchen witch. Take the following keys with you as you go.

+ When claiming the title "witch," you embody all the positive associations with the word: the healer, the outcast, and the rebel.

+ The methods we use in witchcraft are effective because they are passed from one witch to another across time and space, but your intuition is important, too

+ Kitchen witchcraft supports self-care by showing you how to eat nourishing foods, giving you an opportunity to connect with the present moment and encouraging creativity.

+ Emphasize self-care in your practice by remaining open-minded, setting intentions, doing what feels good, developing long-term health habits, and recording your progress.

+ As you clean, prepare, cook, and eat your food, focus on your intention to transform your life in the way you want.

CHAPTER 4

THE HEALING TOOLS OF A KITCHEN WITCH

Every craft requires tools and materials. In kitchen witchcraft, these are likely things you already have or regularly buy, such as your cooking equipment, your dishes, and the food items that stock your pantry and refrigerator. However, you may not be looking at them with the eyes of a kitchen witch.

In this chapter, you will learn how to prepare your kitchen for magic by balancing the energy, cleaning physically and energetically, organizing your tools, and setting up an altar for your practice. You will find information about the ingredients you use, such as herbs and seasoning, vegetables, fruit, and grains. The section about your cookware and serving dishes highlights the pots and pans, spoons, a mortar and pestle, and dishes and their magical symbolism. Then you will explore what's beyond the walls of your kitchen as you learn about the four elements, the moon, the planets, and the seasonal changes. You can also make use of additional healing tools, such as candles, crystals, and essential oils.

Prepare Your Kitchen for Magic

Before doing intentional magic in your kitchen, such as cooking a magical meal, you will want to prepare this space for sacred usage. This means you are setting apart the room or certain areas of it to honor your spiritual practice and your intention to take care of yourself.

As a kitchen witch, you should prepare your sacred space with mindfulness and intention. Start by looking around your kitchen and making sure it is clean and uncluttered. Then organize your tools, setting them up in a way that makes them easily accessible. Finally, create an altar or shrine, placing special items on it that hold personal meaning.

By taking these steps, a kitchen witch can create a space that is conducive to working magic. The more comfortable and familiar you are with your surroundings, the easier it will be for you to tap into your power and work your spells.

Take a Mindful Look Around

When you are next in your kitchen, audit it for energetic imbalances. Stand or sit as close to the middle as you can and take in the entire space. Notice the emotions that come up as you spend time in the kitchen. Like all spaces, the kitchen can become a repository for the thoughts, moods, emotions, and energies that occur within it. This is especially true for a kitchen that hasn't been intentionally used for magical purposes or one that hasn't been energetically cleansed for a while.

Balance the energy of your kitchen by bringing in representations of all four Western elements: the refrigerator is air, the stove is fire, the sink is water, and the ingredients and tools are earth. Here are some other ways to incorporate the elements:

Candles: all four elements, but mostly fire

Color: green or brown for earth, yellow or purple for air, red or orange for fire, blue or pink for water

Crystals and stones: strong earth energy; depending on the type, they also have additional elemental energies associated with them

Plants: earth, air, and water

Start with a Clean Space

For hygienic reasons, it's important to keep your kitchen clean. For magical purposes, you will want to cleanse the energy of the kitchen. Three simple ways to ensure the energy is fresh and ready for any magical working is to declutter, sweep, and cleanse.

Start by straightening the countertops, tables, and other visible surfaces in your kitchen. This should be done daily if possible, and is especially important before you begin preparing a meal.

Sweep the floor daily to move energy around and prevent it from becoming stagnant. If possible, keep a specific broom in your kitchen (and the other rooms of your home) to prevent mixing energies. Some witches also like to use a ceremonial broom that doesn't touch the floor and is strictly for energetic cleansing.

Finally, cleanse the energy with smoke from incense or a smoldering bundle of herbs. If you prefer, you can use sound or a cleansing spray to cleanse the space. When you cleanse the energy, be sure to open a window to allow the unwanted energy a way out.

Organize Your Tools

If you've never taken the time to organize your kitchen for efficiency and flow, this is a good time to do so. Go through your kitchen gadgets, pantry items, refrigerator, cooking tools, spice cabinet, and everything else to determine what is used regularly, what can be thrown or given away, and where it makes the most sense to keep things.

Make sure you do this with a magical eye. If you are coming from another ritualistic practice or are new to witchcraft, thinking about everyday objects like a knife, cup, or pan as magical may seem odd. However, every object is ordinary until the witch assigns it a purpose.

Treat your kitchen herbs and spices with respect. Honor them by keeping them neatly stored in a clean cupboard or drawer away from sunlight and moisture. Turn their labels so you can find what you need easily. Finally, take inventory of the herbs and spices you have and use frequently and learn about their magical properties.

Create an Altar or Shrine

As previously mentioned, the entire kitchen is, in many ways, an altar or a shrine. However, it may not be possible to always maintain your entire kitchen as a sacred space. For this reason, you may want to set up a small reminder of your practice in your kitchen and maintain it as an altar or shrine.

Find a small section of counter space, hang a shelf on an empty wall or over a doorway, hang a series of baskets from the ceiling, or bring in a small table. Here you can keep the tools and materials that reflect who you are and how you practice. This might include statues, symbols, or pictures of your ancestors, household spirits, deities you work with, or any other important aspects of your beliefs.

The Importance of Your Ingredients

The most important part of any witchcraft practice is the intention you put behind it, but the quality of your ingredients is important, too. Try to choose ingredients and prepare meals that keep the result as close to the source as possible.

To do this, seek out locally available food and eat seasonally as much as possible. When your food is grown locally, it means that it is more likely to be ripened on the plant rather than in transportation. This also helps you remember that you are part of the natural world and the solar cycle.

Additionally, how the food is prepared changes the way it makes you feel, and nutrition is complex. For example, certain nutrients are available in the raw version of a food and diminished when cooked. In other cases, nutritional and digestive benefits are increased through the cooking process.

As a kitchen witch, you may wish to start a garden. Whether you have space in a backyard or a sunny windowsill, you can grow some vegetables and/or herbs to use in your healing witchcraft practice. Create a comfortable place to be near your plants and make a habit of observing them each day.

One reason to grow a garden is because it ensures that your magic goes into every step of the process: from sowing seeds to making a meal. As you put your personal energy and focus into growing plants, you develop a deep relationship with your plants and a greater understanding of how they enhance your magic.

Gardening is also an excellent opportunity to connect with the natural world. As you tend to your plants, you become more aware of how they grow and change throughout the year. You learn when to fertilize, water, and cover to protect from cold or heat, and when to harvest the produce. This reflects on how you can take care of yourself at different times of the year as well. In this way, your garden can become a mirror for your self-care practice.

Herbs and Seasonings

Herbs and seasonings add flavor to the meal. The word "herb" is often used in witchcraft to describe anything that comes from a plant, but in culinary terms, it refers to the green and leafy parts of the plants. Seasonings—or spices—tend to come from the seeds, bark, roots, and other parts of the plant. The following list contains common herbs and seasonings, their elemental and planetary correspondence, and their magical association.

Basil: air and fire; Mars; clarity, prosperity, strength, sympathy

Bay: fire; Jupiter and Sun; healing, psychic ability, success, wishes

Black pepper: fire; Mars and Saturn; banishing, protection

Cardamom: air and earth; Venus; clarity, love, relaxation

Chocolate: fire; Saturn; friendship, grounding, love, prosperity

Chile peppers: fire; Sun; amplification, enhancing, protection

Cilantro/coriander: fire and water; Mars and Venus; healing, love, protection

Cinnamon: fire; Jupiter and Sun; abundance, connection, protection, success

Cloves: air and fire; Sun; confidence, money, protection

Cumin: fire; Saturn; loyalty, protection, warding

Fennel: air and fire; Mercury; clarity, communication, protection

Mustard (seed and prepared mustard): fire; Mars and Sun; courage, faith, success, warding

Nutritional yeast: earth and water; Moon; happiness, healing, love

Oregano: air; Mercury and Saturn; courage, joy, justice, letting go, warding

Paprika: fire; Sun; enhancing, personal energy

Red pepper flakes: fire; Mars; protection, romance, strength

Rosemary: air, earth, fire, and water; Mercury and Sun; focusing, healing, mental health, purification

Sage: air, earth, fire, and water; Jupiter; cleansing, healing, purification, wisdom, wishes

Salt: earth; Saturn; cleansing, healing, prosperity, protection

Sugar: earth; Venus; attraction, grace, love, wisdom

Tarragon: fire; Sun; calming, compassion, confidence, personal power

Turmeric: fire and earth; Mars; healing, protection, strength, vitality

Thyme: water; Mars and Moon; cleansing, courage, healing, loyalty, prosperity

Vanilla: water; Venus; comfort, happiness, love, restoration

Tea Leaves

The word "tea" typically refers to plant parts brewed in boiling water. Technically speaking, tea comes from the tea plant or *Camellia sinensis*. Listed below are different varieties of tea that are distinctive in taste and magical properties. The order is from most processed to least.

Black tea: air and fire; Mars; abundance, consciousness, courage, stimulation

Green tea/matcha: earth and fire; Sun; cleansing, health, longevity, love, passion

Oolong tea: earth and water; Venus; balance, divination, love, reflection, serenity

White tea: air and water; Moon; blessings, clarity, divination, new beginnings, protection, vitality

Herbal tea is more accurately called an herbal infusion or perhaps a potion. It is prepared by steeping any edible plant part in boiling water. The magical use of an herbal infusion depends on the herbs chosen. Common herbs include:

Borage: air; Jupiter; courage, inspiration, psychic abilities

Calendula: earth; Saturn and Sun; connection, protection, wishes

Chamomile: air and fire; Sun; abundance, healing, openness

Echinacea: earth and fire; Saturn; connection, enhancing, healing, prosperity

Ginger: earth and fire; Mars and Venus; confidence, prosperity, sensuality, success

Hibiscus: water; Venus; divination, dreams, love

Lavender: air and fire; Mercury; calming, peace, purification

Lemongrass: air; Mercury and Moon; cleansing, healing, opening

Mints: air and fire; Mars and Mercury; concentration, passion, purification

Rooibos: fire; Sun; energy, grounding, peace, rejuvenation, resilience

Rose petals: earth and water; Moon and Venus; divinity, love, peace, relationships

Rosehips: earth; Venus; good luck, healing, love

Vegetables

"Vegetable" is not technically a botanical word. It is used almost exclusively in reference to food to describe the edible part of the plant. That means vegetable is a very broad category of leaves, stems, roots, tubers, bulbs, and flowers that may be eaten raw or cooked. In general, a vegetable is savory. In the list below, you will find some common vegetables, the corresponding element, and the magical uses.

Arugula: air; Mercury; energizing, cleverness

Avocado: water; Venus; abundance, beauty, love, lust

Beet: earth; Venus; blood substitute, love

Bell pepper: earth and fire; Sun and Venus; creativity, energy, love (association depends on the color)

Broccoli: earth; Jupiter and Saturn; protection, spirituality

Cabbage: water; Mercury and Moon; abundance, cycles, luck

Carrot: fire; Mars; abundance, lust

Cauliflower: water; Venus; regulates emotions, glamour, protection

Celery: air and water; Mercury; lust, mental clarity, psychic abilities

Cucumber: water; Moon; chastity, fertility, healing

Garlic: fire; Mars; banishing, courage, protection, purification, warding

Kale: earth; Saturn; healing, prosperity, releasing

Lettuce: earth and water; Moon; divination, prosperity, protection, sleep

Mushrooms (all types): earth; Saturn; healing, protection, psychic abilities

Onions (all types): fire; Mars and Moon; banishing, endurance, prosperity, stability

Potato: earth; Saturn and Sun; healing, luck, protection, self-esteem

Sweet potato: earth; Venus; friendship, harmony, grounding, nurturing, sensuality

Tomato: water; Jupiter and Moon; love, prosperity, warding

Zucchini: fire; Sun; lust, prosperity, protection

Fruits

"Fruit" is a botanical term to describe the portion of the plant that holds the seeds. When talking about food, however, many items that are technically fruits are classified as vegetables, such as tomato and zucchini. In terms of food items that are classified as fruit, we are discussing plant parts that are sweet or sour and fleshy. They are often eaten raw.

Apple: water; Moon and Venus; healing, love, vitality, witchcraft

Banana: water; Jupiter; abundance, fertility, lust, protection

Blueberry: earth; Saturn; protection, warding, wisdom

Cherry: fire; Mars; attraction, love, stimulating

Coconut: earth; Moon; protection, purification

Elderberry: air and water; Venus; astral travel, balance, healing, spirituality

Grapefruit: water; Jupiter and Sun; cleansing, confidence, healing, purification, strength

Lemon: air; Mars and Sun; enhancing, relationships, strength

Lime: water; Sun and Venus; love, peace, protection, relaxation

Mango: fire and water; Jupiter; harmony, relationships, spirituality

Orange: air; Moon and Sun; divination, emotional expression, happiness

Peach: water; Sun; healing, longevity, softens interactions

Pineapple: fire; Jupiter; luck, prosperity, releasing

Pomegranate: air and fire; Saturn and Venus; luck, wealth, wisdom, wishes

Raspberry: earth; Venus; love, luck, protection

Strawberry: water; Venus; abundance, healing, romance

Watermelon: water; Moon; all-purpose, emotional healing

Grains

Grains are the fruit of grass plants. Before the development of agriculture, humans hunted and gathered all the food necessary to survive. When the gatherers found a way to plant the grains that were previously gathered from far and wide, human life became much more stable and rooted in place. Because of this, and the fact that grains are considered the base of the meal, the magical association tends to be about stability, abundance, and security.

Grains can be processed in a huge variety of ways and prepared in many forms. Some grains can be pulled directly from the plant and boiled in water and eaten. Some can be dried, crushed, mixed with water, and other ingredients, then heated to make breads, crackers, cookies, and more. Some can even be eaten raw. Whatever form they are eaten in, they provide a foundation to build flavors from.

Barley: earth; Saturn and Venus; healing, love, protection

Buckwheat: earth; Jupiter; prosperity, protection

Corn: fire; Jupiter; divination, luck, protection, spirituality, warding

Oats: air and earth; Venus; abundance, love, healing, new beginnings, strength

Rice: air and water; Moon; abundance, blessing, prosperity, security

Wheat: earth; Jupiter and Mars; abundance

Protein

Protein is an important nutrient that enables your body to grow and repair tissue and maintain the hormone and immune systems. This building block is made up of amino acids. The human body requires twenty different amino acids for proper function. Animals, including humans, can create eleven of these, but the other nine must be included in the things we eat.

Animal products provide complete proteins. Eating a variety of plants can also provide your body with all the amino acids it needs. Diet is a personal choice, and no matter the source of your protein, it can be incorporated into your witchcraft practice. The recipes in part 2 of this book have been designed and tested for a vegan diet. I hope you will try them as written, but you should also feel free to make substitutions to suit your dietary preferences and health needs. The list below includes some excellent sources of protein, their element and planet correspondence, and magical uses.

Beans (general): air; Mercury and Venus; protection, growth (association depends on the color)

Beef/vegan beef substitutes: earth; Mars and Moon; emotional expression, passion

Butter/vegan butter substitutes: earth; Jupiter; spirituality

Cheese/vegan cheese substitutes: earth, Saturn; all-purpose

Chia seeds: earth and water; Saturn; cleansing, healing, protection, warding

Chickpeas: fire and water; Sun; balance, creation, energy, healing, strength

Egg/vegan egg substitutes: water; Moon; divination, healing, protection, sex, spirituality

Flaxseed: water; Moon; growth, new beginnings, potential

Green peas: earth; Venus; abundance, love, togetherness

Hemp seeds: water; Moon and Saturn; divination, love, mindfulness

Lentils: water; Moon; healing, nourishing, peace

Peanuts and peanut butter: air and earth; Venus; creation, energy, stability

Pistachios: earth; Saturn; change, evolution, growth

Pork/vegan pork substitutes: fire; Jupiter; good luck, longevity, prosperity

Poultry/vegan poultry substitutes: fire; Sun; healing, personal energy

Pumpkin seeds: earth and water; Moon; cycles, life and death, protection, spirituality

Quinoa: water; Saturn; grounding, healing, protection, warding

Seafood/vegan seafood substitutes: water; Moon; cleansing, purification

Sesame seeds and tahini: fire; Mars; abundance, passion

Soybeans, tofu, and tempeh: air; Mercury; fertility, harmony, protection

Sunflower seeds and sunflower butter: fire; Sun; energy, power, protection, wisdom

Walnuts: air; Jupiter; blessings, divination, wishes

Yogurt/vegan yogurt substitutes: water; Moon; spirituality

Liquids

As discussed in chapter 1, the development of the cooking pot allowed early humans to cook food uniformly in liquid, usually water. There are many ways to incorporate liquid into a recipe. The list below includes several commonly used liquids and how they are used for magic and culinary purposes.

Aquafaba (a vegan substitute for egg white made from the liquid in a can of chickpeas): water; Moon; balance, creation, healing

Coconut oil: water; Moon; purification, protection

Coffee: fire; Mars and Saturn; amplifies intention, removes blockages, work ethic; a splash of coffee (or tea) won't drastically change the flavor and can add magical benefits to the meal

Fruit juice: carries the elements, planetary associations, and magical properties of the fruit; use for smoothies or drink on its own, add to the cooking process for flavor or to add the magical properties

Liquid smoke (a condensed form of woodsmoke used for flavor): fire; Jupiter and Mars; amplifying, enhancing

Maple syrup: earth; Venus; attracting, healing, protection

Milk/vegan milk substitute: water and the elements, planetary associations, and magical properties of the base; adds creaminess to soups and sauces; use for smoothies or drink on its own

Olive oil: fire; Sun; fertility, healing, peace, protection

Soy sauce and liquid aminos: earth and fire; Saturn; banishing, enhancing, protection

Stock and broth: water and the elements, planetary associations, and magical properties of the ingredients; amplifies intention and boosts and balances flavor

Vinegar: fire; Mars; banishing, protection, warding; acid balance for salad dressings, soups, and sauces

Water: water; Moon; magical properties from charging with moonlight, crystals, or herbs

Cookware and Serving Ware

Up to this point, you've learned about preparing the kitchen as a sacred space and the various food items you might incorporate into your magical meals. This section is about the tangible tools you can use for your kitchen witchcraft practice as you seek healing. With these essential tools, you'll be able to create all kinds of magic in your kitchen.

In other paths of witchcraft that you may be familiar with, you use ceremonial tools, such as the cauldron, besom, chalice, wand, and athame. Recall from chapter 3 that kitchen witchcraft is a type of folk magic, in which you use the things you have available to you. The cauldron is replaced with your everyday pots and pans, your kitchen broom is your besom, measuring cups and spoons serve as the chalice, the wand is replaced with stirring utensils, and knives act as an athame.

It's important to remember that the tools you use may seem mundane, but in the hands of a kitchen witch, the ordinary becomes extraordinary!

Pots and Pans

The cauldron is a classic symbol of the witch. This imagery became especially well known from the Shakespeare play *Macbeth*. In one of the most famous scenes, three witches stand over a cauldron creating a potion made of ghastly ingredients.

Interestingly, words such as "eye of newt" and "wool of bat" were not meant to be taken literally. These are folk names for common herbs that you can easily find today. Eye of newt is actually mustard seed, and wool of bat is simply holly, nicknamed because of the leaf's resemblance to a bat wing. Regardless, this famous scene, where three witches chant "double, double toil and trouble" over their cauldron solidified the modern image of a witch for generations.

While in the past it was common throughout Europe to cook using a large cauldron hung or placed over a pile of smoldering coals, it is not practical for a modern witch to attempt this. A set of pots and pans of varying sizes is symbolic of the traditional cauldron.

As food containers, pots and pans are aligned with the receptive energy. This balances well with the active heat it receives from the stove top. Together, the fire and water transform the contents from raw ingredients to cooked food.

Spoons and Spatulas

Consider your stirring spoon or spatula to be your wand. The wand is associated with the active energy of fire. Like the stove top, it helps balance the energy of the food within your passive pots and pans. As you stir the content, the heat is distributed, and the ingredients are less likely to burn. The direction you stir is based on your intention. Stir deosil (clockwise in the Northern Hemisphere, counterclockwise in the Southern Hemisphere) to increase something in your life, and the other direction—or widdershins—to decrease something in your life.

The wand is also used to focus and direct your personal energy into a specific area or direction. Use your kitchen utensil to direct your focused intention into the food you are preparing.

Mortar and Pestle

When I got my first mortar and pestle, it made me feel more like a witch than any other tool I had purchased for myself. There is something magical about grinding your own nuts, seeds, herbs, and spices. Perhaps it's the additional personal energy you are putting into the materials you're using. There's no shame in using a food processor, though.

Symbolically, the mortar and pestle represents the balance between active and passive energies. The mortar is the receptacle for the ground material and the pestle actively works to create it. Together, a transformation occurs.

When using this tool, the movement is like that of stirring. If your intention is to use this material in a spell or ritual for increasing, grind deosil. If your intention is to use this material in a spell or ritual for decreasing, grind widdershins.

Cups, Plates, and Bowls

The way you present your magical meal can be as important as the way you prepare it. Take pride in the hard work you put into creating complex food from simple ingredients. Instead of slopping everything together, arrange it attractively. Use garnishes, drizzle the sauce, display your art using the dish as your canvas.

Cups, plates, and bowls are receptive tools, as they hold and contain the magic of the food. Cups and bowls are more aligned with the water element, and plates are aligned with the earth element. Any dish is suitable for the purpose of holding and presenting your food. If you are looking to purchase new dishes, look for some that are made from natural materials and especially clay pottery.

Stay Attuned to the Natural World

At this point, I want you to know that your kitchen witchcraft practice does not need to be contained in the kitchen or even inside your home. In this section, you will learn about the various intangible tools or correspondences that exist outside: the four elements, the phases of the moon, the planets and astrological signs, the seasons, and the solar festivals.

As a kitchen witch, one of the most important things you can do for self-care and healing is to stay tuned in to the natural world. The basis for all witchcraft practices is a connection to nature, this remains true for the specific path of kitchen witchcraft. The following topics are energies you can align with to enhance the magic you are cooking up. They are called correspondences because the energy exists in the spirit realm and you can correspond with that energy by using material representations of them (such as the tools and materials discussed previously in this chapter) to anchor them in the physical realm.

The Elements

The four elements mentioned in this book come from the ancient Greeks who believed air, earth, fire, and water to be the components of all experiences. In their belief, these elements are not only the building blocks of all matter, but also how they thought about health and spirituality as well.

Air: clarity, communication, education, mental health, travel

Earth: career, material objects, money, practical matters, stability

Fire: courage, creativity, motivation, personal power, transformation

Water: divination, emotions, healing, love, new beginnings

Every tool and material that you will use for kitchen witchcraft corresponds with one or more of these elements. Every intention you focus your magic into can be linked with one of these four elements. Part of the magical process is to determine whether you wish to create a harmonious balance with all four or lean into one or two more than the others to overcome feelings of lack.

The Phases of the Moon

You are likely aware that the moon changes phases over the course of about a month. The simplest way to work magic in alignment with the lunar cycle is to increase, invite, and grow during the waxing half and to decrease, banish, and reflect during the waning half. You can also align more fully with this cycle through observing the eight phases, listed here from the beginning of the cycle to its culmination:

New moon: blank page, fresh start, new beginnings, set intentions

Waxing crescent: momentum, motivation, take action now, willingness

First quarter: challenges, decisions, inspiration, nurture your dreams

Waxing gibbous: adjust, create change, edit, refine

Full moon: celebrate your blessings, clarity, peak energy, transition

Waning gibbous: enthusiasm, express gratitude, reflection, storing

Last quarter: forgive, let go, release, remove obstacles

Waning crescent: recuperate, rest, surrender, take time out

You can incorporate the lunar cycle into when you cleanse and/or charge your tools and materials. You may wish to time your spells and rituals around the phase that is most aligned with the intention.

The Planets and Astrological Signs

For the purposes of this book, I have included the seven celestial bodies regarded as planets in classical astrology. You will find in the list below the day of the week and the zodiac sign(s) that the planet rules over. One way to work with the planets in kitchen witchcraft is to plan your menu, self-care activity, or domestic task based on the planet or the zodiac sign that corresponds with the day of the week. Some ideas are listed below.

Sun: Sunday; Leo; employment, health, personal development; spend time with friends/family, tend to plants

Moon: Monday; Cancer; biological cycles, emotions, reflection; clean the bathroom, do laundry

Mars: Tuesday; Aries and Scorpio; courage, sexuality, strength; do handicrafts, get a massage

Mercury: Wednesday; Gemini and Virgo; communication, receiving messages, travel; run errands, sweep/vacuum

Jupiter: Thursday; Pisces and Sagittarius; abundance, success, wisdom; financial planning, make an offering

Venus: Friday; Libra and Taurus; beauty, love, pleasure; get a manicure/pedicure, go on a date

Saturn: Saturday; Aquarius and Capricorn; banishing, boundaries, patience; big projects, energetic cleansing

The Seasons

There was a time when humans were more in tune with the agricultural timing of the seasons. Crops were planted in the spring, they grew to maturity throughout the summer, harvest occurred in the fall, and the winter was a time to rest and prepare for the next cycle. Most modern people are not preoccupied with the growth cycles of plants, especially if you aren't a farmer or gardener. However, a kitchen witch who is striving to eat seasonally and align with the natural world will pay attention to the subtle seasonal changes.

Something to consider is the fact that the Gregorian calendar shifted the beginning and ending of the four seasons to occur at what was once the midpoint of the season. It is interesting to shift this back in your mind and view the middle of the Gregorian season as the beginning of the next season instead. Additionally, depending on your latitude, these dates might not align perfectly with what you experience. Feel free to adjust as necessary. (NH = Northern Hemisphere, SH = Southern Hemisphere)

Imbolc: the first of February (NH) or August (SH); first day of spring; plant metaphorical seeds of new beginnings throughout the spring

Beltane: the first of May (NH) or November (SH); first day of summer; nurture the seeds and help them grow throughout the summer

Lughnasadh: the first of August (NH) or February (SH); first day of fall; express gratitude for the product of your nurturing throughout the fall

Samhain: the first of November (NH) or May (SH); first day of winter; take a break to reflect on what you've learned throughout the winter

The Solar Festivals

As mentioned in the previous section, the Gregorian calendar shifted the seasons to begin on the solar festival dates listed below. However, the solar festivals are the peak of the season, a time that is most like the expected conditions of that season. While the dates listed above mark the beginning of one season (and the end of the previous), the following list of dates mark important transitions in the solar energy. (NH = Northern Hemisphere, SH = Southern Hemisphere)

Yule: the twenty-first of December (NH) or June (SH); winter solstice; shortest day of the year, transition from decreasing to increasing sunlight; time to heal

Ostara: the twenty-first of March (NH) or September (SH); spring equinox; equal amounts of night and day, noticeable increase of warmth and light; time to take root

Litha: the twenty-first of June (NH) or December (SH); summer solstice; longest day of the year; transition from increasing to decreasing sunlight, time to celebrate

Mabon: the twenty-first of September (NH) or March (SH); fall equinox; equal amounts of night and day, noticeable increase of cold and darkness; time to reflect

Numbers

In most world cultures, numbers are deeply symbolic. In witchcraft, you can enhance and clarify the flow of energy toward your intention through taking an action a specific number of times or adding a certain number of ingredients. Using the number two for example: you can light two candles, chant words two times, add two bay leaves, stir the soup two times, cast the spell two days in a row, make the tea at 2:00 p.m., cook the meal on the second day of the month, and so on. The list below includes the magical association of the numbers one through nine.

One: assertiveness, independence, leadership, self-care, willpower

Two: balance, compromise, harmony, partnership, relationships

Three: collaboration, communication, creativity, inspiration, structure

Four: healing, motivation, protection, stability, transformation

Five: change, conflict, destruction, fluidity, risk-taking

Six: celebration, community, family, generosity, hope

Seven: choice, connection, introspection, patience, spirituality

Eight: discipline, personal development, power, prosperity, wealth

Nine: accomplishment, completion, evolution, gratification, transformation

Additional Healing Tools

Most of the discussion in this chapter has been focused on the everyday tools and materials you probably already have in your kitchen. You also learned about the energies of the natural world you can access and anchor into your spells with physical representations.

Now, you may want to consider including some items that conjure a more magical aesthetic into your home and your practice. Below you'll find a discussion about several additional healing tools: incense and candles, crystals and stones, and essential oils. These healing tools work to aid you in your pursuit to balance and restore your personal energy. Energy that flows freely through and around your physical body can help you feel a sense of peace, calm, and equilibrium.

Incense and Candles

Incense and candles are two of the most frequently used tools in witchcraft. They can be used to cleanse an area, set the mood, or attract positive energy. Choose incense in a scent that matches your intention.

For candles, select the size, wax type, and color based on how you will use it. Bigger candles, such as the ones that come in jars, are good for multiday spells and ambience. A small candle, like the kind you put on a birthday cake, burns out more quickly and is great for a quick spell or making a wish.

Black: banishing, hiding, protection

Blue: communication, focus, forgiveness

Brown: blessing, grounding, stability

Green: growth, healing, prosperity

Orange: creativity, justice, vitality

Pink: compassion, receptiveness, self-improvement

Purple: independence, spirituality, wisdom

Red: confidence, motivation, passion

White: all-purpose, cleansing, youth

Yellow: flexibility, happiness, persuasion

Crystals and Stones

Crystals and stones are another popular tool for kitchen witches. They can be used for practically any purpose. Each stone has its own unique properties that can be harnessed for your specific needs. The following list includes some common ones, the element and planet they correspond with, and their magical associations.

Amazonite: earth; Mercury; balance, calming, inspiration

Amethyst: air, earth, fire, and water; all planets; protection, purification, spirituality

Aventurine: air and fire; Mars and Mercury; growth, increasing, abundance

Citrine: fire; Sun; abundance, emotional balance, energy cleansing

Moonstone: water; Moon; intuition, inspiration, receptivity

Onyx: earth and fire; Mars and Saturn; banishing, encouragement, strength

Quartz (clear): air, earth, fire, and water; all planets; amplifying, enhancing, healing

Quartz (rose): earth and water; Venus; compassion, opening, self-esteem

Sodalite: water; Jupiter; expression, focus, guidance

Tigereye: earth, Saturn; balance, creativity, grounding

Essential Oils

Essential oils are plant extracts—herbs, flowers, resins, and roots—produced by steam or water distillation, which is the process used with most essential oils, or cold pressing (expressing), as in the case of citrus oils. They have both medicinal and magical properties and are used in a variety of ways in the witchcraft world: in ritual baths, as an alternative to incense, as fragrance worn on the body, and for anointing candles, to name a few.

Essential oils can be incredibly useful in kitchen witchcraft but using them can be dangerous. They are extremely concentrated and not designed for consumption, so do not use them in place of herbs or other ingredients in your recipes. The consequences of ingesting essential oils can be quite severe. They range from immediate symptoms, such as burning in the throat, abdominal pain, nausea, and vomiting to long-term effects, like serious damage to the liver, gallbladder, and digestive organs. Some oils can even cause heart attacks or death.

When using essential oils in kitchen witchcraft, it's best to diffuse them for their aromatherapeutic benefits. Always keep essential oils out of reach of children and pets. Consult with your veterinarian about whether it is safe to use essential oils around your pets; some animals are especially susceptible to their harmful effects because their bodies process toxins differently, and some essential oils are more toxic than others.

For healing and self-care purposes or when anointing yourself for ritual, it is generally safe to apply essential oils to your skin so long as they are diluted in a carrier oil, such as almond, coconut, or olive oil. Without dilution, some oils can cause burning, desensitization, and even liver damage over the long term.

The Magic Lives within You

Here we are at the end of part 1, and you have come a long way. At this point, the most important thing I want you to remember is that the magic lives within you, and it's just waiting for you to call it for a purpose.

You have learned about the magic that is found in the air we breathe, the water we drink, and the earth we stand on. You hopefully understand that magic is found in the simple things, like the upside-down world you can see in a dew drop on a blade of grass early in the morning. It's important to recognize that these things make up the "craft" part of the word "witchcraft."

You, my friend, are the witch. You, as a unique, living, and breathing human, hold magic of your own to make changes in your life.

As a kitchen witch, remember that the best magic is the kind that you make yourself. With your own two hands, you can create potions and charms that are infused with your own unique energy. You don't need expensive ingredients or fancy tools. All you need is your knowledge, insight, curiosity, and dedication to your craft. When it comes to healing and self-care, remember that the most important tool you have is yourself. The magic is within you. Let it flow through you and into the world.

Key Takeaways

Your success as a kitchen witch will depend on your ability to pay attention to the natural world and use the tools at your disposal to create healing magic. In this chapter, you explored the wealth of ingredients, tools, and correspondences that you can use in your practice. Remember that the most important tool you have is yourself, so stay curious and dedicated to your craft to create powerful kitchen magic and absorb the following points on your way into part 2.

✦ A sacred space is a room or area that is set apart to honor your spiritual practice and your intention to take care of yourself.

✦ It's important to choose ingredients and prepare meals that keep the result as close to the source as possible.

✦ The tangible tools of kitchen witchcraft are the everyday items you likely already have that you give purpose to.

✦ As a kitchen witch, one of the most important things you can do for self-care and healing is to stay tuned in to the natural world.

✦ You are magical.

PART II

Healing Spells, Remedies, and Rituals for the Kitchen Witch

In each of the following eight chapters, you will find spells, remedies, and rituals to be conducted in the kitchen in pursuit of caring for the various areas of your life. You'll learn to be more mindful of the present moment and to express gratitude for the blessings in your life. You'll understand the expansive power of love as you see yourself as someone who is worthy of love and care through the eyes of the people you have relationships with. You'll discover both how to anchor your consciousness into your physical body and how to release yourself from the physical into the spiritual realm. You'll explore your personal energy and creativity and begin to understand the spectrum of human emotions.

CHAPTER 5

SELF-CARE FOR YOUR MIND

As previously mentioned, caring for your mind can help you cope with the stresses of life. This chapter includes a ritual for encouraging mindfulness and four recipes for improving your brain health and supporting overall mental health.

For these spells and recipes, be sure to be mindful and present throughout the process. As you collect and prepare the ingredients, pay attention to the thoughts that enter your mind. Be aware of these thoughts and try not to cast judgment on them. After you finish eating or drinking, record your experience in a grimoire or in the margins of the recipe. Take some time to meditate or journal about the thoughts you recall entering your mind.

Mindfulness Tea Ritual

*Each morning when I sit down to drink my first cup of tea, I practice what
I call my "tea in ten" ritual. This ritual is a type of focused meditation in
which you concentrate only on one task: drinking your cup of tea. You could
implement the procedure for this ritual while eating a meal as well.*

Drinking tea is a form of meditation, a way of releasing the cares
of the day, allowing a sense of accomplishment and satisfaction to
embrace you. Tea invites you to employ all your senses. The gentle
bubbling sound of a water kettle, the feel of holding a warm cup, the
visual delight of the diffusion of color, the fragrance, and the taste—
all are parts of the wonder of tea.

For this ritual, try any of the tea recipes throughout this book,
make a blend from another recipe, or use a premade blend of loose or
bagged tea and/or herbs. Purchase tea, herbs, or herbal blends from
an herb shop or grocery store.

Give yourself at least ten minutes to sit with your tea and drink
intentionally.

Freshly brewed cup of tea
Journal or grimoire
Writing tool

1. Sit at a table or counter with your cup of tea in front of you.

2. Look at your cup of tea. How would you describe the color of the
    liquid? Are there any bubbles? What do you notice about the design
    of the cup? Is steam rising from the top? Can you see any patterns or
    shapes forming in the steam?

3. Place your hands on either side of the cup. Is there a handle? How
    does the cup feel? Is the cup warm or hot from the tea? Is the cup
    smooth or textured?

4. Lift the cup toward your mouth. What does the weight feel like in your hands? How does the motion of the cup change the liquid inside? Do you notice any steam?

5. Hold the cup under your nose and let your lips part slightly. You might close your eyes. What does the tea smell like? Can you sense the temperature of the liquid on your face?

6. With your eyes open or closed, take a sip of the tea and hold the liquid in your mouth before swallowing. What is the taste? How does the temperature feel on your lips and inside your mouth? When you swallow, how does it feel in your throat and body?

7. Lower the teacup back to rest on a flat surface. What sound does it make as it touches the surface?

8. Keep your hands on the cup or rest them in your lap. Do you feel different after one sip? How?

9. Continue observing and sensing the experience as you enjoy your cup of tea. Anytime an unrelated thought enters your mind, acknowledge it, and return your attention back to the cup in front of you.

10. Finish drinking your tea and then reflect on your experience. Pay particular attention to how you felt before starting this activity and how you feel afterward. Record this in your grimoire.

Clari-TEA

Did you know Greek scholars wore wreaths of rosemary on their heads during examinations? They believed this would help their memory, quicken their senses, and increase concentration. During Victorian times, the "Language of Flowers" referenced this practice when stating that rosemary represents remembrance. Additionally, rosemary is a common ingredient in cures for headaches and relieving stress around the world. For these reasons, one of the main ingredients in this iced tea is rosemary.

This tea can be served hot or iced, but you'll find instructions for the iced method below. Your brain is in many ways a data-processing machine. While your brain doesn't literally get hot when it's overworked in the same way a machine does, it can still benefit from a cold drink to cool down when it is overworked.

I chose to use white tea leaves for this recipe because the light flavor blends nicely with the rosemary and blueberry. Additionally, white tea is associated with wisdom, cleansing, and freshness. White tea can be expensive and hard to find, so feel free to omit it or make substitutions as needed. Oolong is also associated with wisdom, green tea is associated with the conscious mind, and black tea is associated with alertness.

This recipe also features blueberries, which have brain health properties as well. You can learn about them in the recipe for the Brainiac Walnut and Berry Salad (page 70).

BLUEBERRY SIMPLE SYRUP

½ cup blueberries (fresh or frozen)
½ cup water
½ cup maple syrup

ROSEMARY-INFUSED WHITE TEA

2 tablespoons white tea leaves
1 tablespoon minced fresh rosemary and a rosemary sprig
  for serving
4 cups filtered water

1. In a saucepan over medium-high heat, combine the ingredients for the blueberry syrup, stir, and bring to a boil.

2. Reduce the heat and simmer for 15 minutes. Occasionally stir the mixture deosil seven times while visualizing yourself with a clear mind and good mental health.

3. Pour the mixture into a glass jar with a lid. Optionally, use a fine sieve to strain the syrup first, pressing the berries to release all the liquid.

4. Add the white tea leaves and rosemary to a tea strainer.

5. In a kettle or small saucepan over medium-high heat, heat 1 cup of water to 185°F (if you don't have a thermometer, bring 1 cup to a boil and add ¼ cup of cold water). Remove from the heat.

6. Place the tea strainer in a teapot or a large mug and pour the water over the tea blend. Steep for 10 minutes. Visualize your intention for a clear mind infusing the water as you watch the color spread from the tea strainer.

7. Remove the tea strainer and pour the hot tea into a quart jar. Add the remaining water.

8. Pour the tea into tall glasses of ice, mix in blueberry syrup to your desired sweetness, and garnish with a sprig of fresh rosemary.

9. Drink the tea and visualize yourself with a clear mind and good mental health.

Harmonious Mind Tacos

The base of this recipe is a type of legume called a lentil. Small and disc shaped, the lentil is packed with beneficial nutrients. It's a major source of protein, fiber, calcium, and several important vitamins and minerals. Among these is tryptophan, an amino acid that increases serotonin levels, which creates a sense of calm and well-being. This is the scientific reason behind the magical use of lentils for bringing peace and harmony. Additionally, lentils hold a deep ancient magic because they have been a food source since the Stone Age.

When determining the magical property of a material, it is useful to consider the way the plant behaves in nature. Red onion and purple cabbage are on the ingredient list because of the high concentration of antioxidants found in red, purple, and blue plants.

An antioxidant is a component that protects an organism from free radicals, a by-product of the metabolic process. Your body has a built-in system for combating free radicals, but you can boost the effectiveness of this system by ingesting foods that have a higher concentration of antioxidants. Plants also need to protect themselves from free radicals, so many plants have developed defenses. One defense is a class of pigments called anthocyanins, which result in the beautiful spectrums of red-blue-purple colors we see in plants.

The purple cabbage has another magical purpose beyond adding antioxidants to the dish. For as long as humans have observed plants, people have used their appearance to determine their healing properties. This concept is often called the "doctrine of signatures," but the belief existed long before Dioscorides began writing about it in ancient Rome. The connections people drew between plant and medicinal properties were not always accurate. For example, cabbage may not heal neurodegenerative diseases, but this plant does hold some mental health magic through the connection drawn by many people in the past.

PURPLE CABBAGE SLAW

1 cup shredded red cabbage
1 cup shredded carrot
Juice of 1 lime
1½ teaspoons extra-virgin
  olive oil
Salt
Freshly ground black pepper

LENTIL TACOS

1 tablespoon coconut oil
½ cup chopped red onion
1 garlic clove, minced
1 cup vegetable broth
½ cup lentils
1 tablespoon fajita seasoning
6 taco-size soft corn tortillas
½ cup salsa
Cilantro (optional)

1. In a large bowl, combine the cabbage, carrot, lime juice, and olive oil and toss well. Season with salt and pepper to taste. Chill until ready to serve.

2. In a medium lidded saucepan over medium-high heat, warm the coconut oil. Add the onion and garlic and cook for 6 to 8 minutes, or until the onion and garlic are lightly browned and tender.

3. Add the broth, lentils, and fajita seasoning and bring to a boil. Stir deosil seven times to combine.

4. Reduce the heat, cover, and simmer for 20 to 25 minutes, or until the lentils are tender.

5. Uncover the pot and slightly mash the lentils. Cook for an additional 6 to 8 minutes, or until thickened.

6. In a dry skillet over medium heat, warm the tortillas, about 2 minutes per side.

7. Spoon the lentils into the tortillas and top with the salsa and slaw. Garnish with fresh cilantro (if using).

8. Eat the tacos while visualizing yourself with a harmonious mind and balanced thoughts.

Brainiac Walnut and Berry Salad

In the health and wellness industry, there is a lot of talk about the term "superfood." This is a label slapped onto a specific food item based on a single nutrient that it contains. This creates a perception that this food is superior and all other foods should strive to be like it. For the most part, buzzwords surrounding health and wellness are simply marketing. Yet, if ever there were a food that deserves a title such as "superfood," I think it would be the blueberry. Blueberries have an incredible concentration of different types of anthocyanins, which translates to a higher concentration of antioxidants than any other food, and a greater potential to enhance your brain's health.

The blueberry is also one of very few native fruits in North America. It was very special to the Native Americans of the Pacific Northwest, who called them "star berries" due to the perfect five-pointed star that forms at the blossom side of the berry. In magic, the star—or pentagram—symbolizes human consciousness. Each point represents one of the four elements, and the fifth point represents the human spirit.

This recipe also features walnuts. You may have noticed that a whole walnut resembles a brain. Walnut is a rare example of a plant listed in the doctrine of signatures (see Harmonious Mind Tacos, page 68) that actually helps the thing it resembles. Walnuts have the magical connection between brain health and mental capacity, with scientific research to back it up. The main reason walnuts benefit your brain is their high concentration of omega-3s and other fatty acids, which keep the cell membranes in your brain healthy.

BALSAMIC VINAIGRETTE

¼ cup extra-virgin olive oil

2 tablespoons balsamic vinegar

2 teaspoons maple syrup

¼ teaspoon salt

¼ teaspoon pepper

SALAD

1 cup walnuts

6 cups assorted greens (arugula, spinach, romaine, etc.)

¼ cup thinly sliced red onion

1 cup fresh blueberries

1. In a glass jar, combine all the ingredients for the vinaigrette and shake vigorously before use.

2. Heat a dry skillet over medium heat. Add the walnuts and toast until aromatic and lightly browned. Shake the pan occasionally to prevent burning. Remove the walnuts from the pan and set them aside to cool.

3. Tear the greens into bite-size pieces and mound them in a shallow bowl or salad plate.

4. Sprinkle each serving with the red onion, blueberries, and toasted walnuts and toss to combine. Drizzle the vinaigrette over the salad before serving.

5. Eat your salad while visualizing your brain getting stronger and more capable of thinking critically.

Mercurial White Bean Soup

Great northern beans are a key ingredient in this. They were chosen for their size, texture, and ability to hold their shape in soup, but you can feel free to replace them with another white bean, such as cannellini or navy beans. White beans correspond with the air element and the dominion of Mercury, especially discovery and insight.

This soup plays with color by using red onions instead of yellow onions in the mirepoix (mix of aromatic vegetables that form a base flavor for a recipe) and purple kale instead of green kale. Feel free to use yellow onion or green kale (such as curly leaf), which have their own health benefits, but the purple color adds a certain aesthetic to the soup that is quite striking.

Purple also increases the overall concentration of anthocyanins in the meal, which are powerful antioxidants that can prevent neurodegenerative diseases. You can read more about this in the recipe for Harmonious Mind Tacos (page 68). In magic, purple is associated with the third eye, which is the gateway to the subconscious mind and wisdom.

1 tablespoon coconut oil
1 medium red onion, chopped
1 garlic clove, minced
2 celery stalks, finely chopped
1 carrot, peeled and finely chopped
¼ teaspoon red pepper flakes
Salt
Freshly ground black pepper
1 bunch purple kale, stems and leaves separated and
   chopped, divided
1 sprig fresh rosemary, leaves removed and minced
2 teaspoons tomato paste
4 cups vegetable broth
1 can great northern beans, drained and rinsed

1. In a large soup pot over medium heat, warm the oil. Add the onions and cook until they are translucent, stirring occasionally.

2. Add the garlic, celery, carrot, and red pepper flakes and season with salt and pepper.

3. Stir occasionally and cook for about 5 minutes, or until the vegetables soften and become fragrant.

4. Add the kale stems, rosemary, and tomato paste. Stir to combine and cook another 2 minutes.

5. Add the vegetable broth and beans and stir to combine. Turn the heat to medium-high and bring to a boil.

6. Reduce the heat and simmer for about 18 minutes, adding the kale leaves toward the end.

7. Season to taste with salt and pepper and serve.

8. Eat your soup while visualizing yourself becoming more insightful and intuitive.

CHAPTER 6

SELF-CARE FOR YOUR BODY

This chapter is about caring for your body and feeling connected to your physical existence. This chapter includes one ritual to support you as you discover what could benefit from healing, as well as send healing energy to that area. You'll also find four recipes designed to help you feel grounded within the vessel that houses your consciousness and your spirit.

Grounding is a practice of connecting with the earth as you release your unwanted energy and refresh it with beneficial energy. It can be done through visualization, breathing exercises, touching the ground with bare skin, physical activity, engaging all your senses, and eating something filling. As you develop a healthy relationship with the things you are eating and drinking for nourishment, it may be helpful to let go of any unhealthy beliefs you have surrounding diet and your body.

Grounding Body Scan

This visualization will give you the opportunity to bring awareness to each of your body parts. In doing so, you can observe whether there is pain, tension, or other signs of needing care. Spend as much time with each body part as you'd like, witnessing their existence, and observing and inviting both sensation and lack of sensation equally. Feel free to modify to match your comfort and physical ability, and wiggle, rotate, shake, rock, or otherwise move the body part as you become aware of it. Don't forget to breathe.

You don't need anything but your body for this process but feel free to light candles and/or incense, hold crystals, diffuse essential oils, play music or calming sounds, or otherwise set the mood for your comfort.

1. Sit or lie down on the floor, making sure your spine is neutral and long. Close your eyes if you like.

2. Notice the parts of your body that are contacting the ground. Become aware of this connection between your body and the supportive earth. Allow your body to sink deeper into the ground, resting and relaxing. As you do, imagine the earth rising to meet you, lifting you as you relax.

3. Visualize the energy in your body. Bring your attention to your toes. Expand your awareness to both feet. Consider the arches, the top and the bottom. Move up to the ankles and the heels.

4. Bring your attention to the shins and the calves. Move on to the knees and the back of the knees. Notice your thighs, the hamstrings and quads, and the sides of your upper legs.

5. Explore your pelvic region. Draw your awareness to the belly and how it moves with your breath. Notice the lower back. Consider the organs inside.

6. Move up to your chest, feel your heart beat, listen to the breath in your lungs. Explore your shoulders and the weight on your shoulder blades.

7. Follow the energy down your arms, through the biceps and triceps. Bring your awareness to the elbow in the front and back. Notice your forearms and your wrists. Pay attention to the space in the palm of your hand. Move to your thumbs and fingers, each joint, pad, and nail.

8. Ease the energy back to your throat and the sides and back of your neck. Bring awareness to your jaw and chin and tongue. Notice your nose, your ears, and your eyes. Feel the back of your head and become aware of your own brain. Pull the energy to the top of your head, feel the spaciousness of your mind.

9. Zoom out as you become aware of your entire form. Observe how it is complete and whole. Remember your connection to the earth beneath you.

10. Open your eyes slowly when you are ready.

Gravi-TEA

Rooibos, also known as red tea or red bush tea, is not technically a tea as it doesn't come from the Camellia sinensis *plant. Rather, it comes from the* Aspalathus linearis *shrub that is native to the west coast of South Africa. Because it is not a true tea, this drink is caffeine free. The name is true to the color, this tea turns a gorgeous reddish-brown drink when brewed. In addition to the wonderful earthy flavor, the color contributes the grounding magic of the earth element in this tea.*

Rhizomes (belowground, horizontal stems) such as ginger and turmeric are also featured in this tea. Ginger adds a spicy flavor. Turmeric has a subtler ginger-like flavor, but its main purpose is to add the vibrant yellow color. Including these rootlike plants in your diet can create a connection in your mind about rooting yourself to the present moment, to the earth, and into your body. Another ingredient—cardamom—belongs to the same botanical family as the others. Cardamom comes from a seedpod and finishes the flavor profile with a somewhat sweet, peppery citrus flavor. Ginger, turmeric, and cardamom are all thought to improve digestion and soothe upset stomachs.

I've included oat milk to make this a tea latte (and for its magical association with strength). I have found that oat milk is the best plant-based milk for frothing. Feel free to experiment with other milk alternatives. If you prefer to skip the latte aspect, simply replace the oat milk with an equal amount of water and stir instead of whisking or frothing.

3 cups oat milk, divided

4 teaspoons rooibos tea

½- to 1-inch piece turmeric root, peeled and thinly sliced
  (or 1 teaspoon turmeric powder)

1- to 2-inch piece fresh ginger, peeled and thinly sliced

1 tablespoon maple syrup

½ teaspoon ground cardamom

¼ teaspoon ground cinnamon (optional)

1. In a small saucepan over medium-high heat, combine 2 cups of oat milk, the rooibos, the turmeric, and the ginger. Bring the mixture to a simmer.

2. Remove the saucepan from the heat and whisk in the maple syrup and cardamom. Let the mixture sit for 5 to 10 minutes, depending on how strong you want the flavor to be.

3. Pour the mixture through a fine sieve into 2 mugs to separate the solid parts from the liquid.

4. Rinse the saucepan and heat the remaining 1 cup of oat milk over medium-low heat. Bring to a simmer but not a boil.

5. Use a frother or a whisk to froth the milk before gently pouring it into the mugs. Garnish with the cinnamon (if using).

6. Drink your tea while visualizing your energy cycling through your body, leaving through your tailbone, and returning refreshed.

Comforting PB&J Oatmeal

Part of caring for the body is instilling a feeling of safety and security. For me, this means reminding myself of my childhood, which was a time when I had fewer worries and responsibilities. When I was a kid, nothing could beat a peanut butter and jelly sandwich at lunch, and I continue to love PB&J as an adult.

This oatmeal is a new take on an old classic. If you've never tried toasting the oats in oil before adding water, it is a real game changer. I was never excited about oatmeal until I started doing this. In magic, oats represent strength and healing.

Something I was really surprised to discover about peanuts is that they form underground. They are part of the legume family, but instead of the seed pods hanging from the stems like you would see with beans and peas, the plant sends what's called a peg under the soil and then the peanut begins to form. Because of this, peanuts represent stability, connection to earth, and opportunity in magic.

For the jelly, I prefer raspberry jam. The color red is important to the magic because it represents primal energy, which means emphasizing your basic physical needs for survival. The abundance of seeds amplifies your intention. The taste is certainly an important factor as well.

As you make and eat this recipe, recall a time in your life when you felt comfortable and safe in your body. Visualize yourself in that space again.

2 tablespoons coconut oil

1½ cups steel-cut oats

4½ cups water

¼ cup smooth natural peanut butter

2 tablespoons raspberry jam

½ cup roasted, salted peanuts, chopped

1. In a medium saucepan over medium-high heat, warm the oil. Add the oats and stir frequently to toast until fragrant and golden brown.

2. Add the water and stir to combine. Bring the mixture to a boil.

3. Reduce the heat and simmer, stirring often, for 8 to 10 minutes, or until the mixture thickens.

4. Remove from the heat and stir in the peanut butter.

5. Serve the peanut butter oatmeal in bowls. Top with the jam and sprinkle with the peanuts.

6. Eat your oatmeal while visualizing yourself in a place where you feel safe and protected.

Grounded Roasted Roots Bowl

This recipe is so good, we have it about once a week in our house. Seriously, the number of times I've made this recipe made it hard for me to recall the proportions because creating it has become second nature.

The reason I included this recipe in the section about self-care for the body is because the main event is the roasted root vegetables. The theme of this chapter is groundedness, and one of my favorite ways to ground myself is by eating something filling. When you are full, you are reminded of your bodily presence. Your consciousness and spirit are housed in a physical body. Additionally, the root vegetables grow within the protection of the earth. They are literally rooted in the ground, and that symbolism carries into the food.

The base of the recipe is quinoa. This is the grain-like seed of a plant that is native to the South American Andes. Quinoa has many potential health benefits due mainly to the fact that it is a good source of magnesium and several other nutrients and is high in protein and insoluble fiber. Magically, quinoa is associated with grounding, healing, and protection. As a seed, it also has magical properties associated with seeds such as beginning anew.

The dressing for this bowl is made using tahini, a paste made from sesame seeds. Some people find it to be a slightly bitter flavor, but it is balanced with the sourness of lemon and the saltiness of liquid aminos. This dressing is so easy and so delicious, you'll want to eat it by the spoonful.

TAHINI DRESSING

2 tablespoons tahini

¼ cup freshly squeezed lemon juice

2 tablespoons liquid aminos (or soy sauce)

VEGGIE BOWL

1 cup quinoa
1½ cups vegetable broth
5 red potatoes, chopped
2 medium beets, peeled and
  chopped
5 radishes, chopped
1 tablespoon and 1 teaspoon
  extra-virgin olive oil, divided

Salt
Freshly ground black pepper
1 bunch curly leaf kale
1 teaspoon freshly squeezed
  lemon juice
1 tablespoon sunflower seeds
1 tablespoon pumpkin seeds

1. Preheat the oven to 425°F. Line a baking sheet with parchment paper.

2. In a jar, whisk all ingredients for the tahini dressing with a fork until blended. Add water to thin as needed. You can also use a small blender to make the dressing.

3. Cook the quinoa according to the package directions, using the vegetable broth in place of water.

4. In a large bowl, combine the potatoes, beets, and radishes with 1 tablespoon of olive oil, ¼ teaspoon salt, and ¼ teaspoon pepper. Stir to coat.

5. On the prepared baking sheet, arrange the vegetables in a single layer. Place in the preheated oven and roast for 20 minutes or until the potatoes are fork-tender. Stir halfway through.

6. Remove and discard the kale stem. Place the leaves in the bowl used for the vegetables and drizzle with 1 teaspoon of olive oil. Gently massage the kale to soften and tear the leaves into bite-size pieces. Add the lemon juice, the sunflower seeds, the pumpkin seeds, and a pinch each of salt and pepper. Toss to combine.

7. Serve the quinoa topped with the roasted vegetables and the kale salad. Drizzle with the tahini dressing.

8. As you are eating, visualize your body growing heavier and more connected to the physical realm.

Strengthening Chocolate Mousse

You'll notice aquafaba listed in the ingredients below. This is the liquid that accompanies a can of beans, specifically chickpeas. Instead of calling it "canned bean water," it is named using the Latin words for these things, which sounds more appetizing, if you ask me. Whenever I open a can of chickpeas, I pour this precious liquid into a clean ice cube tray and freeze it for later.

Surprisingly, this viscous liquid that most people pour down the drain foams in a way that is almost indistinguishable from egg whites. It takes about ten minutes for the peaks to form. Be sure all tools that will encounter the aquafaba are very clean. Any grease or fat will prevent the peaks from forming.

Chickpeas, and by extension, the water they come with, are magically associated with strength, balance, and healing. For this recipe, they support the chocolate, which is associated with grounding and balance. Chocolate is brown, a color associated with earth magic, stability, and groundedness.

You can eat this mousse by itself or add your favorite toppings like raspberries and hazelnuts, Connected Coconut Cream (page 96) and chocolate shavings, or blueberries and mint. Choose toppings that are associated with your magical intention.

1 cup vegan chocolate chips
¾ cup aquafaba
¾ teaspoon apple cider vinegar

1. Fill a small saucepan with about 1 inch of water and bring it to a boil over medium-high heat. Reduce the heat so the water is at a steady simmer.

2. Place the chocolate chips in a glass or metal bowl that is larger than the saucepan. Place the bowl on the rim of the saucepan and stir the chocolate chips deosil until smooth. Set aside.

3. In a mixing bowl, combine the aquafaba and apple cider vinegar. Use a whisk or hand mixer to whisk the aquafaba until it forms stiff peaks. As you whisk, visualize your body being healthy and as strong as a mountain. Continue whisking for another 2 minutes.

4. Add the slightly cooled chocolate to the aquafaba and continue to mix. It will be runny at first and will begin to thicken; become aware of your own physical form as the mousse thickens.

5. Divide the mousse into four ice cream bowls and chill for at least 2 hours.

6. Eat the mousse while visualizing yourself protected in a fortress of rocks and mountains.

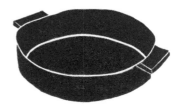

CHAPTER 7

SELF-CARE FOR YOUR SPIRIT

This chapter includes a ritual for spiritually cleansing your kitchen and four recipes for helping you feel more connected with the divine energy that exists both inside and outside you. When it comes to caring for your spirit, it seems abstract because the spirit is not tangible. The ingredients chosen for these recipes *are* tangible, so the connection is more symbolic than what you saw in previous chapters.

The main consideration is that these food items are light. In contrast to the previous chapter, where many of the foods and ingredients were specifically designed to pull you into your physical body, these foods are meant to help you disconnect from the physical realm as you explore the spiritual realm. In this way, they are more prayerful and ritualistic.

Kitchen-Cleansing Ritual

In chapter 4, you learned briefly about cleansing the energy in your kitchen. Cleansing is the act of removing unwanted energy from a person, place, or object so they can't harm, disturb, or hinder you.

There are many methods for energy cleansing. The procedure below uses smoke from a smoldering bundle of dried herbs. You can use practically any herb for cleansing because the smoke is doing the work (be sure to research whether their smoke is toxic or otherwise harmful). Using herbs that are associated with spirituality—such as lavender, holy basil, culinary sage, mint, thyme, or rosemary—would give an additional boost to the process. You can purchase these from witchy small businesses or make one yourself by tying together fresh herbs and letting them dry completely.

You will be invited to begin at a doorway and walk deosil around the space. If your kitchen has more than one entry, begin at the doorway you use most frequently. The energy of the natural world is thought to flow in the deosil direction, so walking this way brings your space into alignment with the natural flow.

You will also be invited to chant a cleansing mantra as you go. There is an example of something you might say, but feel free to speak to the spirit of your kitchen and speak intuitively about your desire to cleanse the space. It's okay to say nonsense, to sing, to shout, to whisper, or to not say anything at all.

It is good practice to cleanse at the changing of the seasons (four times a year), but feel free to cleanse your space more frequently if the energy begins to feel stagnant or uncomfortable. Open the windows and outward-facing doors, if possible, to allow unwanted energy to leave.

Matches or lighter
Bundle of dried herbs
Small bowl or large shell
Folding hand fan (optional)

1. Light your herbal bundle. Use the bowl to catch falling ash.

2. Begin chanting a cleansing mantra, repeating it as you go. For example: "I release the bonds that hold stagnant energy in place."

3. Start in the doorway and move in a clockwise direction through the room.

4. Use the fan (or your hand) to waft the smoke into every area of the kitchen. Raise and lower your herb bundle so the smoke travels from floor to ceiling and into every corner and nook.

5. Return to where you began and decide whether you wish to continue cleansing. When you are done, extinguish the herb bundle completely.

Spirituali-TEA

This tea is technically an herbal infusion because it has no tea leaves (and no caffeine). Caffeine has many beneficial properties but being overly alert and hyperaware of your physical presence can inhibit your ability to connect with your spirit. Bringing yourself into a relaxed state is an effective way to open yourself up to spiritual experiences and messages. For this reason, the ingredients in this tea are thought to be relaxing and are often used just before bed in preparation for sleep.

One such ingredient is chamomile flowers, which come from several plants that belong to the aster family. The most cultivated and sold species are English or Roman chamomile (*Chamaemelum nobile*) and German chamomile (*Matricaria recutita*). While different plants, they have very similar medicinal and magical properties. Due to chamomile's resemblance to the sun, many historical cultures associated it with their sun deity and everything within its dominion. Additionally, it has protective and purifying energy, which is useful when exploring the realms of the unknown.

Another calming ingredient is lemongrass. In addition to its bright, lemony flavor, this plant can invite spiritual messages to reveal themselves to you and is very helpful when used before or during divination.

Spearmint is included because, like most mints, it is uplifting and inspiring. In addition to this association, it is protective, specifically in the spirit realm, and it invites only helpful spirits to interact with you.

Finally, vanilla is included in this recipe for comfort. Exploring your spirituality can lead to a feeling of purpose and wholeness. However, the process is not always comfortable. Vanilla is often described as basic, plain, or boring. There is a normalness about the flavor that can be soothing during times of discomfort. Vanilla also adds a smoothing flavor to the overall profile.

Drink this tea before astral projecting, practicing divination, journaling about your beliefs, dreamwork, spiritual meditation, or any other time you wish to connect with your spirit.

3 parts dried chamomile

2 parts dried lemongrass

1 part dried spearmint

1 cup boiling water per serving

½ teaspoon vanilla extract per serving

1. In an airtight container, mix the herbs together.

2. Measure 1 tablespoon herb blend into a tea strainer and place in a mug.

3. Pour the boiling water over the tea strainer and pour in the vanilla. Stir deosil seven times. Steep for 5 to 10 minutes, then remove the tea strainer.

4. Drink your tea while visualizing yourself exploring the spiritual realm.

Connected to Spirit Salad

This chapter is about eating light recipes that help you disconnect from the physical realm to connect with the spirit realm. This salad is uplifting and refreshing, and it's made using ingredients associated with the spirit realm.

The poppy plant is associated with the spirit realm, particularly when it comes to death and remembering loved ones who have passed away. This connection goes back three thousand years to ancient Egyptian funeral rites. Poppies were thought to ensure life after death and safe passage to the land of the dead. In Greek mythology, Demeter transformed her mortal lover Mekon into a poppy when he died, as a symbol of their everlasting love.

Every part of the poppy plant is toxic except for the seeds; therefore, the seeds are the only part a kitchen witch should include in a recipe. They are included in the dressing for this salad. Please keep in mind that the pod that holds poppy seeds is distilled to create opium, which means that eating poppy seeds can trigger a positive result for some drug tests.

Apples have many magical associations. For this recipe, we will focus on their association with witches, divination, and the afterlife. Most people cut apples down the middle along the stem, but if you cut them across the middle at the widest part, you will notice that the seeds are aligned in the shape of a five-pointed star, or pentagram. This symbol is strongly associated with witches and is most often used to represent the four elements plus spirit.

This pentagram symbol is hidden but becomes obvious when you know the secret, which is a wonderful metaphor for divination. Divination is the process of discovering what is unknown through communicating with divinity (whether that divinity is an external or internal force).

For the magical properties of broccoli, see Cleansing Vegetable Soup (page 94).

LEMON POPPY SEED DRESSING

½ cup freshly squeezed lemon juice
½ cup extra-virgin olive oil
¼ cup maple syrup
2 teaspoons Dijon mustard
½ teaspoon salt
¼ cup diced shallot
1 tablespoon poppy seeds

KALE AND BROCCOLI SALAD

2 cups curly kale, stems removed
1 teaspoon extra-virgin olive oil
1½ cups broccoli florets
1 medium apple, cored and chopped
2 scallions, green and white parts, thinly sliced
¼ cup dried cranberries

1. Combine all salad dressing ingredients except the poppy seeds in a blender. Blend until smooth.

2. Pour the blended mixture into an airtight container and add the poppy seeds. Put on the lid and shake to disperse.

3. Refrigerate until ready to use. Use within 5 days.

4. In a large bowl, combine the kale with 1 teaspoon of olive oil. Make the leaves more tender by massaging them, and tear them into bite-size pieces.

5. Add the remaining ingredients to the bowl of kale and toss to combine.

6. Pour the desired amount of lemon poppy seed dressing over the salad and toss to coat.

7. Eat your salad while visualizing your magic swelling within you.

Cleansing Vegetable Soup

This soup continues the theme for this chapter of choosing foods that are light and refreshing when caring for your spirit. It is very cleansing and detoxifying but not in the scammy way the health and wellness industry uses these buzzwords. Your liver, kidneys, and skin are perfectly capable of removing unneeded nutrients and pollutants from your body. No, this soup is cleansing in the spiritual sense of the word.

Broccoli is the main vegetable in this soup. The first symbolic aspect of broccoli is the fact that it comes in "crowns," which is reminiscent of the crown chakra, the energy point associated with spirituality. Interestingly, a broccoli crown is the flowering portion of the plant and is considered the largest edible flower.

Another point of symbolism is the shape of a broccoli floret, which is like a tiny tree. In this way, it represents the tree of life, a symbol that spans cultures around the world. It is interpreted in many ways, such as a connection between the earth and the universe, spiritual growth and rebirth, the unique spiritual path each witch follows, and ancestry.

The mushrooms are also an important ingredient with spiritual symbolism. European folklore tells a story of the faerie ring or a circle of mushrooms that sometimes appears in a field of grass. Different tales give different reasons: the fae danced in circles that wore down the grass, dragon fire burned a circle that allowed mushrooms to pop up, gnomes buried treasure and the mushrooms protected it, and more. Regardless of what you believe, it is unmistakable that mushrooms are magically linked to the spirit realm.

2 tablespoons coconut oil
1 yellow onion, chopped
3 garlic cloves, minced
1 medium carrot, peeled and diced
1 celery stalk, diced
Salt
2 cups sliced cremini mushrooms
2 teaspoons fresh ginger, peeled and grated
2 teaspoons cumin
6 cups vegetable broth
2 cups chopped broccoli florets
1 (15-ounce) can chickpeas
2 cups torn kale leaves
Freshly ground black pepper
1 lemon, cut into wedges

1. In a large soup pot over medium-high heat, warm the oil. Add the onion, garlic, carrot, and celery and season with salt. Sauté for about 3 minutes, or until the vegetables are soft and the onion is translucent.

2. Stir in the mushrooms and sauté for 5 more minutes.

3. Add the ginger and cumin, sauté for 1 to 2 minutes, until fragrant.

4. Pour the broth in and stir to combine. Bring the mixture to a boil. Add the broccoli, reduce the heat, and cook for 5 minutes.

5. Stir in the chickpeas and cook for 5 minutes, or until all the vegetables are tender.

6. Just before serving, add the torn kale leaves and cook until wilted. Season with salt and pepper to taste. Stir soup deosil seven times.

7. Ladle the soup into bowls, with a squeeze of lemon.

8. Eat your soup while visualizing your body removing any energy that is harmful or otherwise unwelcome.

Connected Coconut Cream

This whipped cream is light and airy and comes together very simply. There are just three ingredients that you will whip together: coconut milk, maple syrup, and vanilla. This dessert encourages spirituality for a couple of reasons. It is light, which helps your consciousness exist outside of the physical body. Additionally, consider the crown chakra, or spiritual energy point, that is located on the top of the head. This dessert can be eaten as a topping for other desserts, such as Strengthening Chocolate Mousse (page 84).

The individual ingredients in this recipe have magical and spiritual properties as well. Learn about the magical properties of vanilla in the recipe for Spirituali-TEA (page 90). Coconut milk encourages receptivity due to its association with the moon. It can also offer protection when astral traveling and exploring the spirit realm.

"You'll attract more bees with honey than with vinegar" is a common phrase, and it applies to magic. Sweeteners are attractants. This recipe calls for maple syrup, but you can substitute equal parts of another sweetener. Maple trees are thought to protect against unwelcome spirits and energies, so it is included as a protective measure.

There are a few things to do to ensure success. Make sure you chill the can of coconut milk in the refrigerator for at least nine hours so that it hardens enough to be whipped. You'll also want to chill a bowl and the mixing attachments in the freezer for one hour before whipping. Try not to shake the coconut milk can so that the water and cream remain separated. Reserve the coconut water and add a bit during the whipping process if the cream is too stiff or you see clumps. You can drink what's left or use it in smoothies.

1 (14-ounce) can full-fat coconut milk

1 tablespoon maple syrup

1 vanilla bean, seeds scraped (or ½ teaspoon vanilla extract)

1. Use a can opener to open the cold can of coconut milk from the bottom. Reserve the coconut water for another use (or discard) and scoop the solid coconut cream into a chilled bowl.

2. Use an electric hand mixer to beat the cream until smooth and fluffy.

3. Add the maple syrup and vanilla and mix gently to combine.

4. Cover the bowl and place in the refrigerator until ready to use. It gets firmer when cold but softens at room temperature. Use within 2 weeks.

5. Eat your whipped cream and visualize your connection to the spirit realm becoming stronger.

CHAPTER 8

SELF-CARE FOR DIFFICULT EMOTIONS

The following spells will help you connect with your emotional state through understanding the signals your subconscious mind is sending your conscious mind. These rituals and recipes are designed to help you recognize what emotion you are feeling and process it in a healthy way.

In many ways, these recipes and rituals are aligned with a practice called "shadow work." Shadow work is the process of integrating the darker aspects of the self, including difficult emotions, with the parts of yourself that are easier to love. It is not about lopping off those hard-to-love parts of yourself, but about acknowledging and accepting them as part of your whole authentic self.

Observing Your Emotions

Emotions can be a source of power for your magic, they can be used as fuel for rituals and spells. They can also give you direction by guiding you toward the activities and people that make you feel good and steering you away from what feels unpleasant and harmful. It is very beneficial to a kitchen witch to understand their emotions and what triggers them.

As you go through your day—cooking, cleaning, working, and playing—you will likely experience a range of emotions. This is because you are human. The fact that you can experience such a wide range of emotions is a beautiful thing. It's important to remember that no emotion is more valuable or true than another. The differences lie in the physical sensations they create and whether the experience is pleasant or causes discomfort.

In the same way that you experience your five senses of taste, touch, smell, sight, and sound to help you understand your environment, emotions are simply cues that help you understand your internal world. Your subconscious mind triggers a physical sensation in your body for your conscious mind to interpret as an emotional state.

Most people are unaware of this process happening, so to observe your emotions, you will need to be in tune with your body. This ritual is designed to help you do just that as you tune in to the physical experience and interpret it as an emotion.

Start by getting in the habit of noticing emotions, especially if you were previously unaware of how you feel. As you progress, try to put a name to the sensations that you're having, even if it's not an emotion. If you name it, you can recognize it more easily when you feel it again, which can help you better understand what to do when you experience a difficult emotion.

Additionally, when you have a description of what you are feeling, you can look it up and compare it to how emotions are described in books and articles. This can help you learn to name your emotional sensations.

Timer
Grimoire
Writing tool

1. Set a timer to go off five times in a day.

2. Describe the sensation you are experiencing in your body when the timer goes off.

3. Record your observations. Start by writing "I feel . . ." and see where that takes you.

4. Reflect on whether the feeling is pleasant or unpleasant. Then brainstorm how you can resolve the emotion. Use a divination tool such as the tarot to help you with this if you like.

5. Repeat as frequently as you need to.

Honest-TEA

This is meant to help you be honest about your emotions. It is a true tea because its base is green tea. Green, black, oolong, and white tea all come from the Camellia sinensis *plant. The difference between these different varieties depends on how long the leaves oxidize, where the plant grows, and when the leaves are harvested. Green tea has a shorter oxidation process than black tea, which makes the flavor smoother and the caffeine content lower.*

The importance of green tea in this recipe is the effect it has on emotions. Consuming green tea is thought to increase serotonin and dopamine, which are the "happy" hormones. When you have increased levels of these, you are more likely to feel relief, peace, and contentment.

Chamomile has an effect similar to that of green tea. It is thought to reduce stress and anxiety as it increases blood flow to the brain and blocks the effect of cortisol (the "stress" hormone). Additionally, because chamomile resembles the sun, it can be a symbol of happiness, warmth, and growth.

Calendula is a beautiful orange flower that is sometimes called pot marigold. Like chamomile, it corresponds with the sun. They are both used magically to lift the spirit and show the optimistic perspective so that you can "keep on the sunny side of life."

When a wild rose loses its petals at the beginning of winter, it leaves behind a small, orange-colored fruit called a rosehip. Fresh rosehips are incredibly high in vitamin C. While this is diminished when they are dried, it can still be a good source. It is thought that increasing the amount of vitamin C you consume can improve your mood and reduce feelings of anxiety, depression, and fatigue.

½ cup green tea leaves

¼ cup dried calendula flowers

¼ cup dried chamomile flowers

2 tablespoons dried rosehips

2 cups water

1. In an airtight container, mix all the herbs together.

2. Add 1 tablespoon of the tea blend to a tea strainer.

3. In a kettle or small saucepan, heat the water to 170°F (if you don't have a thermometer, bring 1 ½ cups of water to a boil and add ½ cup of cold water). Remove from the heat.

4. Place the tea strainer in a teapot or large mug and pour the water over the tea blend. Steep for 10 minutes.

5. Remove the tea strainer and serve the hot tea.

6. Drink the tea while visualizing yourself expressing your emotions honestly and processing them in a healthy way.

Optimistic Orange Stir-Fry

Tofu is made by condensing soy milk, which is a liquid made from pureed soybeans and water. Use firm or extra-firm tofu for this recipe. Both usually come refrigerated and packed in water. The first thing to do is to remove as much water from the tofu as possible so the tofu can absorb other flavors. The instructions below for pressing the tofu work great, but if you plan to cook with tofu a lot, I highly suggest investing in a tofu press.

Tofu has a very mild flavor, so the flavor for this dish comes from the ingredients in the orange sauce. The magic also comes largely from the orange sauce. The color orange is used in magic for boldness, vitality, and celebration. It is also associated with increasing joy and excitement in life, attracting opportunities that are aligned with your purpose. It is thought to be an optimistic color that lifts the mood during times of hardship.

This color is also associated with emotional balance. Difficult emotions can block the flow of emotional energy. Eating orange foods—such as orange juice and zest and carrots used in this recipe—can help bring this energy center into balance.

Interestingly, the color orange got its name from the fruit, which contains high levels of vitamin C. Whenever you feel a cold coming on, I bet you pour yourself a glass of orange juice to boost your immune system and try to nip it in the bud. As mentioned in the recipe for Honest-TEA (page 102), vitamin C can improve your mood (and prevent scurvy).

1 cup brown rice
1 (14-ounce) package tofu, drained
⅓ cup freshly squeezed orange juice
1 teaspoon grated orange zest
1 tablespoon soy sauce
2 tablespoons coconut oil, divided
½ teaspoon grated ginger
2 garlic cloves, minced

¼ teaspoon red pepper flakes
1 cup shredded carrot
2 scallions, green parts only, thinly sliced
2 tablespoons chopped cilantro
1 tablespoon sesame seeds

1. Cook the brown rice according to the instructions on the package.

2. Wrap the tofu in several layers of paper towels (or a clean, dry tea towel). Place a cutting board and a stack of 2 or 3 cookbooks on top to press excess moisture. Leave for 30 minutes, then cut the tofu into ½-inch cubes.

3. In a bowl, combine the orange juice, orange zest, and soy sauce.

4. In a medium saucepan over medium-high heat, warm 1 tablespoon of coconut oil. Add the ginger, garlic, and red pepper flakes and cook for about 2 or 3 minutes, or until fragrant.

5. Pour the orange mixture into the saucepan and bring to a simmer. Reduce the heat and simmer for 3 or 4 minutes, or until syrupy. Stir in the carrots and remove from the heat.

6. In a skillet over medium-high heat, warm 1 tablespoon of oil. Add the tofu cubes and cook each side for about 2 minutes or until golden brown.

7. Toss the tofu with the orange mixture.

8. Mound the rice onto plates and top with the orange tofu. Garnish with the scallions, cilantro, and sesame seeds.

9. Eat your stir-fry while visualizing yourself crossing a street to the "sunny side."

Comforting Vegan Mac-N-Yeez

Part of healing through processing difficult emotions is making yourself comfortable and doing things that you associate with happiness. To me, this means making and eating macaroni and cheese. When I was a kid, Kraft macaroni and cheese was one of the only foods I was allowed to make without supervision. A happy memory for me is coming home from school, sharing a blue box with my sister, and giggling together as we decompressed from the challenges of the day. When I decided to switch to a vegan diet, I began my hunt for a simple mac and cheese recipe.

The inspiration for this recipe is from a vegan restaurant in Seattle, Washington, called Plum Bistro. They didn't give me their secret, but I think I've nearly matched their recipe, which I'll share with you, but first, let's discuss the ingredients.

Nutritional yeast, or what my mother-in-law calls "hippie dust," is a deactivated form of *Saccharomyces cerevisiae,* commonly known as baker's or brewer's yeast. It creates umami in vegan and vegetarian dishes with its nutty and cheesy flavor. It is also a good source of B vitamins. Nutritional yeast can be used in magic for improving health and increasing happiness.

This dish is orange due to the presence of nutritional yeast and especially if you use orange vegan cheese. Orange is a color associated with joy, fun, opportunity, and overcoming difficult emotions.

1 pound elbow macaroni

4 cups unsweetened almond milk, divided

3 garlic cloves, smashed

3 sprigs fresh thyme

3 tablespoons vegan butter (such as Miyoko's)

¼ cup all-purpose flour

1 teaspoon apple cider vinegar

Freshly ground black pepper

1 teaspoon salt

1 teaspoon red pepper flakes

½ teaspoon paprika

1 tablespoon stone-ground mustard
1 tablespoon soy sauce
¼ cup nutritional yeast
4 cups vegan cheese (2 8-ounce packages of Violife brand cheddar shreds), divided
¼ cup breadcrumbs

1. Cook the pasta according to the package directions.

2. Preheat the oven to 400°F.

3. In a large saucepan over medium heat, combine 3 cups of almond milk, the garlic, and the thyme. Stir for 7 minutes; do not allow the mixture to boil. Remove from the heat and strain the solids. Set the milk aside.

4. In a large pot over medium-low heat, melt the butter. Add the flour and stir with a whisk for about 1 minute to make a roux. Do not let it brown.

5. Add the milk to the roux and whisk for about 1 minute until smooth.

6. Stir in the final cup of almond milk and the apple cider vinegar and cook for another minute. Season with the black pepper.

7. Add the salt, red pepper flakes, paprika, mustard, soy sauce, and nutritional yeast. Use a whisk to combine.

8. Add the drained pasta and 3 cups of cheese to the pot and fold together to coat the noodles.

9. Pour the mixture into a 3-quart baking dish. Sprinkle the breadcrumbs and the remaining cheese evenly over the top.

10. Place the baking dish in the preheated oven and bake for about 30 minutes.

11. Let rest about 10 minutes before serving.

12. Eat the pasta while visualizing yourself doing something that fills you with joy.

Emotional Expression West African Peanut Stew

This is one of my favorite recipes. You may notice that the ingredients are like those chosen for the recipes in chapter 6, namely that many grow underground. Feel free to use this recipe as a body self-care ritual as well.

One reason I chose to include this recipe in this chapter is because it is orange when cooked. However, the main reason is because I often make it when I am having a hard day. It's simple to throw together, and many of the steps involved are very therapeutic for expressing emotions such as frustration, sadness, and anger.

When you peel the outer layer of the onion, imagine you are peeling away your own tough exterior and exposing your raw emotions. Then, when you begin chopping, allow yourself to cry your eyes out and exaggerate with sobbing noises and wailing. Choose a juicy onion for this recipe to ensure optimal tears.

Get out excess emotions when you peel the garlic. Place the garlic clove between a cutting board and the side of your knife. Use your fist and (carefully) slam it onto the knife to crack the peel. Feel free to shout as your fist hits for an extra release.

You'll also need to peel the sweet potato for this recipe. This is a great opportunity to release the things that you've outgrown. With each scrape of your peeler, think or say something you wish to let go of. Feel free to repeat the same thing. When you are done, you are left with a fresh sweet potato and a fresh start.

1 tablespoon coconut oil
1 onion, diced
3 garlic cloves, minced
1 teaspoon red pepper flakes
1 orange bell pepper, diced
1 sweet potato, peeled and chopped
1 (14.5-ounce) can diced tomatoes
Salt

Freshly ground black pepper

1 teaspoon cumin

1½ teaspoons chili powder, divided

⅛ teaspoon cayenne pepper (optional)

½ (6-ounce) can tomato paste

½ cup natural peanut butter

4 cups vegetable broth

1 (15-ounce) can chickpeas, drained and rinsed

4 to 6 cups collard greens, stems removed, leaves chopped

Fresh cilantro (optional)

Roasted peanuts (optional)

1. In a large soup pot over medium heat, warm the oil. Add the onion, garlic, and red pepper flakes and sauté for about 5 minutes, or until the onion is translucent.

2. Stir in the bell pepper, the sweet potato, and the tomatoes with their juices. Season with salt and pepper, the cumin, ½ teaspoon of chili powder, and the cayenne (if using). Raise heat to medium-high and cook for 5 minutes.

3. Add the remaining chili powder, the tomato paste, the peanut butter, and the vegetable broth. Stir to combine until no clumps of peanut butter remain.

4. Reduce the heat to medium-low and cover the pot. Simmer for 15 to 20 minutes, or until the sweet potato is fork-tender.

5. Stir in the chickpeas and collard greens. Cook until the leaves are wilted.

6. Ladle the soup into bowls and garnish with the cilantro and peanuts (if using).

7. Eat your soup while reflecting on your emotional state as compared to before you started cooking. Consider whether you released what you needed while cooking.

CHAPTER 9

SELF-CARE FOR SELF-LOVE

Loving yourself shows you how you want to be loved by others. Self-care is a form of self-love. When it comes to taking care of yourself, you need to know exactly what you need and when you need it. That is why loving your authentic self is important to self-care.

Authenticity requires a degree of self-knowledge, which allows you to clearly see the parts of yourself you need to love and nurture, and the parts of yourself you need to learn tools to manage and evolve. This chapter includes a ritual for honoring who you are and four recipes for learning how to love yourself.

Kitchen-Enchanting Ritual

Enchanting—or charging—is a practice in which you assign an object or a space a purpose. After cleansing a space (see the Kitchen-Cleansing Ritual, page 88), you leave a void. You want to make sure that space is filled with the energy you want and not more energy that you'll need to cleanse away. This is done with enchanting.

You can charge your kitchen with any intention using a variety of methods. For this ritual, you will be enchanting your kitchen with the intention for self-love. When you enter your kitchen, it will remind you of the commitment you are making to healing your ability to love yourself with kitchen witchcraft.

Choose personal items and activities that remind you that you are divine and worthy of being worshipped, honored, and cared for. The goal is to create an inviting place where you want to spend your time and that fills you with joy. Here are some ideas that you might like to try: move things around, hang art and pictures, paint the walls, play music, hang shelves for displays, bring in plants, place figurines and crystals, sing loudly, hang suncatchers in the window, or dance around. No matter what you decide to do, do so with the intention of making this your happy place.

Whenever you are experiencing low self-esteem and other unhelpful emotions, go to the kitchen and look at the things that make you happy. Repeat this ritual as frequently as you'd like.

Matches or lighter
Candle (pink or your favorite color)
Candleholder
A photo of yourself
Personal items and kitchen decor

1. Light the candle and secure it in the candleholder.

2. Look at the picture of yourself and say:

    I know who I am, and I like who I am.
    I honor who I am today.
    I am proud of my past that led me to this moment.
    I am proud of the potential my future holds.

3. Spend some time making the kitchen your happy place, while the candle continues to burn.

Beau-TEA-ful

This is a version of chai that uses oolong tea instead of Assam black tea. The word "chai" is Hindi for "tea," although the oldest versions of this beverage did not actually include leaves from the Camellia sinensis *plant. The masala (blend of spices) was created for Ayurvedic healing purposes in India thousands of years ago. It was also thought to increase a youthful appearance and elevate the mood.*

Oolong tea leaves are less fermented than black tea and have slightly less caffeine. The flavor is also less tannic for this reason. In magic, oolong tea corresponds with the water and earth elements, which are both passive energies. It encourages love, reflection, and emotional expression.

The rose also corresponds with earth and water, as well as Venus, the planet of all forms of love, beauty, and pleasures. Humans have helped the rose evolve from the unassuming wild bloom to the display of many petals most of us are familiar with today. There was a point in history when a single rose was valued higher than any other material a person could own. This earned the rose the title "Queen of All Flowers." Drink this tea as a reminder to treat yourself like royalty.

Cardamom is another key ingredient in this tea that is often associated with love and beauty. It is a common ingredient in love potions to attract a romantic partner. This is a potion for falling in love with yourself, as you remember all your lovable features.

1-inch cinnamon stick

3 green cardamom pods

2 cloves

1 teaspoon fennel seeds

½ cup water

1 tablespoon oolong tea leaves

½-inch fresh ginger, thinly sliced

2 tablespoons dried rose petals

1 tablespoon sugar, or to taste (optional)

½ cup coconut milk

2 teaspoons rose water

1. Use a mortar and pestle or a spice grinder to crush the cinnamon, cardamom, cloves, and fennel seeds.

2. In a small saucepan, bring the water to a boil. Reduce the heat to low and add the crushed cinnamon, cardamom, cloves, and fennel seeds. Simmer for 3 to 4 minutes.

3. Add the tea leaves, fresh ginger, rose petals, and sugar (if using) and simmer for an additional 3 to 4 minutes. Stir deosil one time and watch the ingredients swirl while visualizing yourself standing in your own power.

4. Pour in the coconut milk, bring the mixture back up to a gentle simmer, and cook for 5 minutes.

5. Pour in the rose water and cook for 2 minutes.

6. Strain the tea into a mug and serve.

7. Drink your tea and visualize yourself surrounded by a glowing pink light. As you continue to drink, visualize the light getting brighter and warmer as you become more capable of self-love.

Heart Beet Burger

My love for burgers didn't begin until after I switched to a plant-based diet, so my judgment on what makes a good burger may not mean much to a nonvegan. That said, this is an excellent burger patty. It stays together when cooked, it has a great texture, and the flavor is yummy.

The main ingredient of this patty is the beet. It gives the burger a beautiful pink color and something to sink your teeth into. In magic, the beet can be used as a substitute for blood magic for obvious reasons. It also represents the heart, so it is a perfect addition to love spells, including self-love.

The way to get the patty to stick together is with the use of "chia eggs." When chia seeds are mixed with water, they form a substance that resembles an egg white. Chia seeds contain omega-3 fatty acids, which are thought to improve cardiovascular health. Because the heart is the energy center for love, a healthy heart leads to healthy love.

Another type of fatty acids are omega-6s, and hemp hearts are a good source for these. However, they are included in this recipe for their name and their shape. Hemp hearts correspond with Venus, the planet of love, but they also correspond with Saturn, the planet of discipline. Self-love is about unconditional compassion for yourself, and it's also about giving yourself rules and respecting yourself enough to follow them.

3 tablespoons chia seeds
½ cup water
¼ cup quinoa
2 tablespoons coconut oil
1 onion, diced
2 garlic cloves, minced
2 cups beets, peeled and grated
2 tablespoons nutritional yeast
Salt
Freshly ground black pepper

⅓ cup hemp hearts
¼ cup pumpkin seeds
¼ cup sunflower seeds
1 (15-ounce) can chickpeas, drained (reserve the liquid)
½ cup panko breadcrumbs
Nonstick cooking spray

1. Make the chia eggs: in a small bowl, combine the chia seeds and the water and set aside for at least 15 minutes.

2. Cook the quinoa according to the package instructions.

3. In a skillet over medium-high heat, warm the oil. Add the onion and garlic and sauté for 3 minutes, or until the onion is translucent.

4. Add the beets and nutritional yeast and season with salt and pepper. Cook for 5 minutes.

5. Add the chia eggs, hemp hearts, pumpkin seeds, sunflower seeds, and ¼ cup of reserved aquafaba to a blender. Blend until smooth. The mixture will be sticky.

6. Transfer the beet mixture to a food processor. Add the chickpeas and blended seed mixture. Blend until combined but not pureed. Add more aquafaba if necessary.

7. Transfer to a bowl and fold in the cooked quinoa and panko bread-crumbs until evenly mixed.

8. Form the mixture into 4 patties and place on a plate. Refrigerate for about 10 minutes.

9. Heat a pan to medium-high heat. Coat the pan with nonstick cooking spray, and then add the patties to the pan. Sear one side for about 5 to 7 minutes, or until browned. Remove the patties, coat the pan again, and sear the opposite side.

10. Toast the buns and assemble the burgers with your favorite toppings.

11. Eat your burger while visualizing your heart growing in its capacity to be compassionate toward everyone, including yourself.

Authentic-Self Salad

Pearl couscous, also known as Israeli couscous, is named for its size and shape, which resembles natural pearls. In nature, pearls are made when certain species of mollusks defend themselves from irritants. The oyster, mussel, or clam coats the polluting particle with layers of a fluid they secrete that hardens into a lustrous pearl. One mollusk's trash is a treasure for a human.

I think the pearl is a beautiful metaphor for self-love. Most people have something about themselves that they feel is flawed, but someone else sees it as unique, endearing, and entirely lovable. To love yourself more, you may need to look at yourself through the lens of someone who loves you.

Additionally, the natural pearl is multilayered, just like you. There is who you are at the surface, the person you present to strangers and acquaintances. There's who you are to close friends and family. There's a layer that you may show to an intimate partner. There's a version of you that you alone know. There's even a layer that exists only in your subconscious. Self-love is a journey of self-knowledge, as you discover these layers and move through the world authentically.

The pearl couscous is a major component of this self-love salad. It also features cherries and tomatoes, which are red, the color of love, and are associated with Venus, the planet of love.

Pistachios are green, which is associated with the heart energy center. Magically, they can be used to break unwanted spells that have been placed on you. This includes the spells you've placed on yourself through negative self-talk and perpetuating beliefs about yourself that are untrue and hurtful.

PEARL COUSCOUS SALAD

1½ cups dry pearl couscous
¼ cup pistachios, coarsely chopped
1 English cucumber, diced
1 pint grape tomatoes, halved
½ cup fresh herbs, such as mint and parsley
¼ cup dried cherries
Salt
Freshly ground black pepper

LEMON VINAIGRETTE

¼ cup freshly squeezed lemon juice
1 garlic clove, grated
1 teaspoon Dijon mustard
¼ teaspoon salt
¼ teaspoon pepper
½ teaspoon maple syrup
¼ cup extra-virgin olive oil

1. Cook the couscous according to the package directions. Drain.

2. In a jar, combine all ingredients for the vinaigrette and shake well.

3. In a dry pan over medium-high heat, toast the pistachios until golden and fragrant. Shake the pan frequently to avoid burning.

4. In a large bowl, combine the drained couscous, cucumber, tomato, herbs, toasted pistachios, and cherries. Season with salt and pepper to taste. Drizzle the vinaigrette over the salad and toss to combine.

5. Eat warm or cool in the refrigerator for later.

6. Eat your salad while visualizing your lustrous layers peeling back to reveal the various aspects of yourself. Acknowledge and accept each one with love.

Venusian Tomato Soup

When Spanish explorers returned from South America, they told the story of the Orinoco River Valley in Venezuela, calling it "the gateway to the Garden of Eden." They brought back many foods and treasures, including the tomato, which has a long history of cultivation in South America before Europeans arrived.

In Europe, the tomato was given names that mean "apple of love" and took on the many magical associations of the traditional apple. It corresponds with Venus, the planet of love, and is thought to protect from unwanted influences. For this reason, I find it to be a wonderful food for developing your self-esteem, resisting negative self-talk, and learning to love yourself.

Additionally, tomatoes are part of a family of plants called the nightshades. Many of the plants in this family are poisonous, which proves your family can be toxic and you can still grow into a lovable person.

This soup features fresh tomatoes and the sun-dried variety, which creates a complex flavor. You can replace the fresh tomatoes with a 28-ounce can of crushed tomatoes to simplify the process. Serve the soup warm or cold depending on your mood, your preference, or the weather.

2 pounds tomatoes (4 to 6 tomatoes)
2 tablespoons extra-virgin olive oil, divided
¼ cup diced onion
1 garlic clove, minced
1 teaspoon cloves
2 tablespoons coconut oil
2 tablespoons all-purpose flour
¼ cup oil-packed sun-dried tomatoes, drained and chopped
2 tablespoons chopped fresh basil and a few whole basil leaves, divided
2 tablespoons freshly squeezed lemon juice
Salt

Freshly ground black pepper
Vegan sour cream, for serving

1. Bring a large pot of water to a boil.

2. Score the bottom of each tomato with an X and add to the boiling water. Boil for about 1 minute or until the skin pulls away.

3. Transfer the tomatoes to a bowl of ice water and let cool.

4. Peel and quarter the tomatoes, then pulse in a food processor to desired consistency.

5. In a skillet over medium-high heat, warm 1 tablespoon of olive oil. Add the onion and sauté until the onion is translucent. Cook longer for a sweeter flavor. Add the garlic and cloves and cook until fragrant, about 1 minute. Remove from the heat and set aside.

6. In a large soup pot over medium heat, warm the coconut oil. Stir in the flour to make a roux.

7. Pour in a small amount of crushed tomatoes and whisk until there are no lumps. Add the remaining crushed tomatoes, the sun-dried tomatoes, and the onion mixture. Stir to combine.

8. Cook until the soup is hot throughout. Remove from the heat and stir in the chopped basil. Season with salt and pepper to taste. Ladle into bowls.

9. In a jar, combine 1 tablespoon of olive oil with the lemon juice. Shake well and drizzle over the soup. Garnish with a few whole basil leaves and a dollop of vegan sour cream.

10. Eat your soup while reflecting on the way you think about and speak to yourself. Let the soup empower you to reframe the negative things that come to mind.

CHAPTER 10

SELF-CARE FOR ENERGY AND CREATIVITY

Your personal energy is made up of the parts of yourself that are not physical but are still recognizable as you, including your emotions, spirit, sense of being alive, thoughts, memories, and beliefs. All of these exist within and around you in an energetic field called the aura. When your aura becomes stagnant, it can block your creative fire and your ability to make magic happen.

Creativity is sparked when your personal energy is flowing freely through and around you. Below, you will find an energy-centering ritual to help you bring your energy in so that you can direct it toward your magical intention and your healing practice. The four recipes in this chapter are designed to give you a boost of energy so that you can get your body moving, the blood flowing, and manifest your creative ideas.

Energy-Centering Visualization

Centering is a magical technique that is essential to self-care. It replenishes your personal energy when it is drawn low and pulls the energy into a focused center that you can direct toward healing or magical intention.

Your center is the place where all your energy radiates from. For me, this is the center of my abdomen. Some people find their energy center at their heart or in the middle of their forehead. Yours may be somewhere else entirely. In the visualization, take some time to discover where this is for you. If you have trouble sensing it, I suggest focusing on the center of your body.

After visualizing your energy, stay in the imagined space for as long as you like. It can be very educational to hang out in your energy galaxy and get a close-up look at your personal energy. You can also discover energy leaks while reflecting and noticing if the energy moves away from your center during the visualization.

You don't need anything for this visualization except your mind. You can light candles or incense, play music or soothing sounds, run an essential oil diffuser, set out or hold crystals, or otherwise prepare your space in a way that sets a comforting mood.

1. Lay down or sit comfortably. Enter a meditative state by focusing on your breathing.

2. Find your center and feel the energy circulating from it.

3. Imagine that you—and your energy center—are the nexus of a galaxy. Orbiting all around you are stars and planets and comets and meteors. These are your energy fragments.

4. Notice that some of the orbits are large, while others are nice and close to the center. Feel the gravity of your center grow and pull the farthest fragments of energy closer to you.

5. Watch the bits of energy move closer to your center as the gravity continues to grow stronger.

6. Ease yourself out of the meditation when you are ready.

7. Record in your grimoire how you feel in contrast to how you felt before you centered. Make note of any observations you made about your personal energy during the visualization.

Creativi-TEA

This tea is meant to boost creativity and energy with ingredients such as green tea, citrus fruit, and cayenne.

Green tea is a true tea that comes from the *Camellia sinensis* plant. The importance of green tea in this recipe is the stable energy it provides. Green tea does contain caffeine. Many people experience the effects of caffeine differently depending on the source. Coffee tends to have a steep increase and an equally steep decline in energy. Tea is usually more gradual and steadier. Because green tea has lower levels of caffeine than black or oolong tea, most people find it to be a more pleasant experience.

You can make this recipe with about 1 cup of any citrus juice that you like. In magic, citrus corresponds with the sun and therefore can be used to encourage happiness and personal strength. I love grapefruit and lemon for this recipe. Grapefruit is used magically for encouraging confidence and mental clarity. In magic, lemons are cleansing and energizing.

In terms of health benefits, citrus fruits have a lower glycemic index score than most other fruits. Foods with a high glycemic index score are the ones that take you on the roller coaster of sugar rush to sugar crash. Foods with a low glycemic index score are less likely to give you a spike in blood sugar because the glucose is released slowly. Additionally, citrus have a high vitamin C content, which is thought to help you absorb other nutrients, such as the antioxidants and caffeine in green tea, more easily.

Finally, the pinch of cayenne pepper is optional, but I like the spicy kick. Cayenne, like most spicy peppers, corresponds with Mars, the planet of energy. Additionally, cayenne can speed up the magical effects of other ingredients that it is mixed with.

2 cups water
2 teaspoons green tea leaves
Juice of 1 grapefruit, seeds removed
Juice of 1 lemon, seeds removed
Maple syrup to taste
Pinch cayenne pepper (optional)

1. In a kettle or small saucepan, bring the water to 170°F (if you don't have a thermometer, bring 1½ cups to a boil and add ½ cup of cold water). Remove from the heat.

2. Add the tea to a tea strainer and place the tea strainer in a teapot. Pour the water over the tea. Steep for 5 minutes.

3. Divide the juice and tea between two large mugs. Stir in the maple syrup and sprinkle with cayenne (if using).

4. Drink your tea while visualizing your personal energy.

Mango, Corn, and Black Bean Salad

These days, fruit in a salsa may not seem surprising to many people, but I remember the first time my grandmother served us pineapple salsa. She went on and on about how creative it was. This inspired her to try many dishes using what, to her, was a new and interesting flavor combination. This memory showed me how using ingredients in unexpected ways can be a muse and spark the creative juices.

This is not the recipe for pineapple salsa but is inspired by it. This recipe has become one of my favorites. You can eat it with tortilla chips or as a filling for tacos or burritos. Try it with Harmonious Mind Tacos (page 68) or the Rainbow Fajitas (page 152), on top of a bed of greens, on a burger (such as the Heart Beet Burger, page 116), or on its own!

Two components of this recipe are corn and mango, which are yellow in color. This color corresponds with the sun and represents imagination, inspiration, and happiness. Yellow is also an energetic color that stimulates your personal spirit.

The dressing for this salad calls for a large amount of cilantro, which can be used in magic to help attune yourself with your soul and your creative spark. The dressing is seasoned with coriander. Did you know that coriander and cilantro are names for different parts of the same plant? Cilantro refers to the leaves and stems, and coriander refers to the dried seeds. In magic, any seed represents new beginnings and ideas.

CILANTRO-LIME DRESSING

1½ cups fresh cilantro

¼ cup lime juice

1 teaspoon maple syrup or agave nectar

1 garlic clove, chopped

½ teaspoon salt

½ teaspoon ground coriander

½ cup extra-virgin olive oil

SALAD

1 (15-ounce) can black beans, drained and rinsed

1½ cups corn kernels, raw or grilled

1 (10-ounce) container cherry tomatoes, quartered

1 avocado, diced

1 large mango, diced

½ red onion, diced

1. Add all the dressing ingredients except the olive oil to a blender. Pulse to combine and chop the cilantro.

2. Add the olive oil and continue processing until smooth.

3. In a large bowl, mix all the salad ingredients.

4. Pour the dressing over the salad and toss to coat.

5. Eat your salad while visualizing yourself becoming inspired. Be very observant of your thoughts, as they may be ideas for a new path to follow toward a career, project, relationship, or another goal.

Energizing Jambalaya

The cultural identity of a recipe can usually be found by looking at the aromatics you add at the beginning. A French mirepoix is made of diced onions, carrots, and celery. If these are minced, you're looking at a soffritto from Italy. Diced onions, peppers, and tomato make it a Spanish sofrito. In this recipe, we have a Cajun blend that's called the "holy trinity": diced onion, pepper, and celery.

In Christianity, the Holy Trinity represents the Father, the Son, and the Holy Ghost—three forms of one being. We see triplets like these in many spiritual belief systems representing three aspects of a being: mind, body, and spirit. The important symbolism of the trinity in this recipe comes from my belief that feeling energetic and creative requires connection with all these aspects of the self. All creations begin in the mind, with inspiration from the spirit and execution by the body.

Additionally, this recipe features some ingredients that correspond with the fire element. Where there's smoke, there's fire! This recipe includes liquid smoke, which is a natural byproduct of condensing the smoke and steam from burning wood. It adds the smoky barbecue flavor, without needing to barbecue. It is available in most grocery stores and a little goes a long way.

The herbs and spices in Creole seasoning correspond with Mars, the fiery planet of motivation and energy, and are thought to be energizing in some way. You can purchase Creole seasoning in a store or make it yourself using ground paprika, black pepper, and cayenne pepper, and dried thyme, oregano, basil, onion, and garlic.

Another fiery herb in this stew is the bay leaf. Cooking with bay leaves adds flavor to the broth but the leaves are not meant to be eaten. In my family, it's good luck if you get the bay leaf in your bowl. When you find the bay leaf, make a wish!

2 ears of corn, husked and halved

1 tablespoon extra-virgin olive oil

1 poblano pepper, seeded and diced

1 onion, diced

1 green bell pepper, diced

2 celery stalks, diced

Salt

Freshly ground black pepper

1 (15-ounce) can dark red kidney beans, drained and rinsed

1 (14.5-ounce) can fire-roasted diced tomatoes with garlic

1 cup vegetable broth

¾ cup long grain white rice, uncooked

1 bay leaf

1½ teaspoons Creole seasoning

½ teaspoon liquid smoke

1 tablespoon flat-leaf parsley, chopped

Hot sauce, to taste

1. In a large pot, cover the ears of corn with water. Bring to a boil and cook for about 5 to 7 minutes.

2. In a large soup pot over medium-high heat, warm the oil. Add the poblano pepper, onion, bell pepper, and celery. Season with salt and pepper and stir deosil three times. Sauté for 5 minutes, or until the onion is translucent.

3. Stir in the beans and tomatoes. Cook for another minute before adding the broth, rice, bay leaf, Creole seasoning, and liquid smoke.

4. Bring to a boil, cover, and reduce heat. Simmer for 20 minutes, or until rice is tender, stirring occasionally.

5. Serve jambalaya in bowls and top with the corn on the cob. Garnish with parsley and sprinkle with hot sauce.

6. Eat while visualizing yourself expressing your creative energy.

Energy Bites

In high school, my friends would get together to watch new episodes of television shows. We would share all kinds of snack food, but there was always at least one tube of cookie dough. The sugar rush would help us stay up late having fun together. I still love cookie dough, but I don't love the sugar crash. The energy in these energy bites is more sustainable because it comes from complex carbohydrates and healthy fats.

The addition of matcha powder adds a small amount of caffeine to the bites. Matcha powder is made when young tea leaves are ground into dust. It has the same magical properties and health benefits of green tea leaves, but it's more concentrated. Plus, the caffeine that comes from tea has a more stable and long-lasting energizing feeling than what you might experience from coffee.

These energy bites are held together with sunflower seed butter. When sunflowers are growing, the flowers always face toward the sun, following it throughout the day. Because of this, the seeds are packed with solar energy. In magic, the sun rules over creativity and personal power.

You can mix in any extra ingredients based on your magical intention and flavor preference. Try dried cranberries and chopped almonds, golden raisins and chocolate chips, or chopped dates and cashews.

2 cups rolled oats
1½ cups sunflower seed butter
1 tablespoon coconut oil
3 tablespoons matcha powder
¼ teaspoon salt
1 teaspoon cinnamon
¼ cup maple syrup
1 cup shredded coconut, unsweetened
1 cup mix-ins (nuts and dried fruit)

1. Preheat the oven to 325°F. Spread the oats on a baking sheet and place in the preheated oven. Toast for 10 minutes, stirring halfway through. Remove the oats and allow them to cool.

2. In a small saucepan over medium-high heat, warm the sunflower seed butter, coconut oil, matcha powder, salt, cinnamon, and maple syrup. Stir constantly until combined and melted. Visualize your creative energy flowing into the mixture as you stir.

3. In a large bowl, combine the cooled oats, the shredded coconut, and the mix-ins and stir well.

4. Pour the melted sunflower seed butter over the dry ingredients and mix with your hands or a wooden spoon.

5. Roll the mixture into balls using about 1 tablespoon of mixture per ball. Place them on a plate and transfer them to the refrigerator. Cool for at least 30 minutes.

6. Store them in an airtight container in the refrigerator for up to 2 weeks or in the freezer for up to 3 months.

7. Eat a bite before pursuing a creative project.

CHAPTER 11

SELF-CARE FOR YOUR RELATIONSHIPS

As humans, community is crucial to our survival. A major component of the human experience is in our communities. It is in our DNA to seek a community of people to travel together in the journey of life.

The rituals and recipes in this chapter are designed to help you find people who have similar values, interests, and concerns surrounding the things you care about and maintain healthy relationships with the people in your community. When properly cared for, a community means you never need to be alone in your sorrow or in your joy. In community, you become aware of and sensitive to the needs of others and can be reminded that there is more than just your own conscious awareness of self.

Boundaries Visualization

In relationships, it's important to have boundaries to protect your energy from being depleted and allow you to maintain your independence. Shielding is one way to create a magical boundary to separate your personal energy from external energy. It doesn't necessarily mean the external energy is threatening or harmful to you, it's just a way to keep your own energy separate and more available for magical working.

Ideally, you would ground (see chapter 1) and center (see chapter 10) before you build a shield.

This visualization guides you through making a shield that resembles a medieval knight's. If this doesn't feel right, feel free to visualize something else. Below are some other ideas for shields you can test that may feel more comfortable or satisfying. Construct them in the same way as illustrated in the following instructions: by visualizing them surrounding you.

A whirlpool or hurricane of water swirling around a calm eye of the storm where you are

Big gusts of wind or a tornado blowing around you and sending away negative energy

A sphere of burning flames to incinerate any negative energy that tries to get close

Mountains of solid, impenetrable rock

A tangle of thorns sticking out away from you, with beautiful flowers on the inside

Clouds of smoke and mist that obscure you from enemies

Anything else you can imagine! Whatever feels right to you.

You don't need anything but your mind for this visualization. You can set the mood using candles and incense, protective crystals, and music, if you'd like.

1. Sit or lie down.

2. Visualize your body surrounded by a sphere of glowing light. Make sure it completely surrounds you with no cracks or weak areas.

3. Imagine the light forming to your body like a second skin. Let it lock into place around you.

4. Visualize the outside of this shield shining and reflective like a mirror.

5. Imagine negative energy coming toward you and bouncing off the mirror back to its sender.

6. Reflect on whether you feel protected and contained. If not, look for weak spots and visualize more protection, or try one of the alternatives in the description above.

Uni-TEA

When it comes to relationships, we all need them. Everyone needs to interact with other humans. This tea is designed to help you fight off infections and soothe a sore throat after long conversations.

Echinacea flowers can be used to help your body fight off bacterial and viral infections. It has a reputation as a cure-all in the world of herbalism. Though the scientific evidence is inconclusive, the association with healing has created a magical link between this flower and healing. When taken as a tea, it has the potential to prevent illness and speed up recovery.

Elderberry (*Sambucus nigra*) is another herb with a long history of use for healing. It is thought to boost the immune system to help fight off infections. In magic, it is associated with the communication energy point in the throat due to its blue color. Use it for protecting against and removing curses or hexes, especially to heal a broken relationship and to help balance emotions after an argument.

The third plant in this herbal blend is peppermint. This plant is great for clearing the sinuses. The Celestial Seasonings plant in Boulder, Colorado, used to do tours. I had a tea mug for years that said, "I survived the Mint Room," which was a favorite attraction for many visitors. Mint has such a strong scent and flavor that they kept it separate from all the other herbs so that it wouldn't affect the flavor of the other teas. Entering the Mint Room would open the entire respiratory system, which is very helpful for communication. In magic, peppermint is cleansing and protective. In this recipe, its role is to make room for new healthy relationships and protect you from harmful ones.

This tea tastes great without a sweetener, but it has a particular magical role to play. Sweetener is literally sweetening. It can be used to make relationships more harmonious and to make you more attractive to the people you want in your life.

⅓ cup dried echinacea flowers

3 tablespoons dried elderberries

2 tablespoons dried peppermint leaves

1 cup water maple syrup

1. In an airtight container, mix all the herbs together.

2. Measure 1 tablespoon of the herb mixture into a tea strainer and place in a mug.

3. In a kettle or small saucepan, bring 1 cup of water to a boil.

4. Pour the boiling water over the tea strainer. Brew for 3 to 5 minutes, then remove the herbs. Add maple syrup to taste.

5. Drink your tea and visualize your throat glowing with blue light. Imagine it feels soothed and relaxed, ready to express your needs in your relationships.

Herby Hummus to Share

Hummus, a spread that originated in Southwest Asia, is made from the base ingredients of chickpeas, sesame seeds, olive oil, lemon juice, and garlic. It is simple to put together, so it is an excellent addition to a party tray. Serve it as a dip with fresh-cut vegetables, such as cucumber, broccoli, carrots, peppers, and tomatoes and with pita chips and olives. Keep leftovers in an airtight container and store in the refrigerator. Eat within a week.

One thing I love about hummus is that it can be customized based on the flavors you prefer, the color association for your magic, and the magical properties of the ingredients. For example, beet hummus is a beautiful magenta color that can be used for love magic, and roasted red pepper hummus has a smoky, energizing flavor. In this recipe, you will use fresh herbs that are common ingredients in green goddess salad dressing: tarragon, parsley, and chives.

Tarragon is perfect for this sharing hummus due to its magical association with being compassionate. It also is thought to bring peace and calm to situations and can help you recognize your sense of self within the larger collective.

In magic, both parsley and chives are used to ward off unwanted spirits. In this hummus, they act as protection for you and your guests against hostile feelings and discord. In this way, the hummus encourages an atmosphere of pleasure and festivity.

1 (15-ounce) can chickpeas, drained and rinsed
¼ cup tahini
¼ cup freshly squeezed lemon juice
2 tablespoons extra-virgin olive oil, plus more for serving
1 garlic clove, chopped
½ teaspoon salt and more as needed
Water (optional)
½ cup fresh parsley, chopped, plus more for serving
¼ cup fresh tarragon, chopped
2 tablespoons fresh chives, chopped

1. Add chickpeas to a food processor and process for about 1 minute. Scrape down the sides of the bowl with a rubber spatula.

2. Add the tahini, lemon juice, olive oil, garlic, and salt to the food processor and process for about 3 minutes, pausing to scrape the sides as necessary. If the hummus is too thick or not blending smoothly, run the processor and slowly add up to 2 tablespoons of water until the hummus is the desired consistency.

3. Add the parsley, tarragon, and chives and process for about 2 minutes, or until combined and smooth. Taste and adjust flavor if desired.

4. Transfer the hummus to a serving dish. Drizzle with olive oil and garnish with fresh parsley.

5. Eat the hummus while visualizing joyful interactions with the people in your life.

Open to Love Fruit Salad

This fruit salad is magically associated with love and openness. It can open you up to new relationships of all types, whether you are looking for new friends, a romance, a business partner, or to reunite with an estranged friend or family member.

Apples are often thought of as a lustful fruit, but they have a round energy that encompasses love of all kinds. One interesting thing about apples is that you can plant the seed of a delicious apple, but the tree that grows from it will not produce fruit that are in any way like the parent. To get an apple that is edible, a small chunk of wood from a tree that produces desirable fruit must be notched into another tree. This is called grafting.

The symbolism of this is what made me want to include apples in this recipe. An individual apple tree cannot produce something desirable. It requires the help of another tree. It is the same for humans. We do better when supported by friends and family members.

Strawberries are perfect for any magic involving love for several reasons. They are heart shaped, a recognizable symbol for love. Make sure you slice them in a way that preserves the heart. They are red, which is a color generally associated with passion, romance, and love. And they are sweet and juicy, both of which are attractants in magic.

Pomegranates correspond with the air element, which helps with communication and authentic expression. This fruit also corresponds with Venus, the planet of love and pleasure, and Saturn, the planet of boundaries and social norms. The edible portion of a pomegranate is the jewellike red cap of the seed, which is called the aril. It takes quite a bit of effort to remove the arils from the fruit, which is a good reminder that relationships cannot be put on autopilot. Maintaining a healthy relationship requires effort from both parties.

I like to add mint to this fruit salad for a bright flavor. It also promotes harmony in a relationship by helping smooth over any hard feelings.

1 cup green apple, cored and diced

1 cup strawberries, hulled and thinly sliced

1 cup pomegranate arils

1 cup blueberries

2 teaspoons fresh mint, chopped

1 tablespoon lime juice

1 tablespoon maple syrup

1. Add the fruit and mint to a large bowl.

2. Drizzle the lime juice and maple syrup over the fruit and toss to combine.

3. Eat your salad while visualizing a relationship in your life becoming stronger.

Courageous Borage Chia Pudding

Chia seeds absorb any liquid they are added to and form gelatinous globs with a texture like tapioca pudding. You can blend it before eating if you prefer a smooth texture. Keep in mind that thinner milk alternatives (such as rice milk) will result in a thinner pudding, and thicker milk alternatives (such as coconut milk) will make a thicker pudding. Use more chia with thin liquids.

You can eat this pudding on its own or layer it as a parfait with fruit (such as the Open to Love Fruit Salad on page 142) granola, and/ or another color of chia pudding (hibiscus makes a beautiful pink pudding).

In terms of magic, chia is associated with protection, cleansing, and healing. For the purposes of this recipe, you can think of it as a palate cleanser. Whether you are looking for new friendships or romances, or want to improve existing relationships, the chia can work toward making a clean start, protecting your vulnerable heart, and healing hurts from the past.

The color of this pudding is a vibrant blue that reminds me of blue raspberry candy. Borage is one of the only truly blue foods, so it's fun to use for the shocking color alone. This shade of blue is associated with the air element, communication, and authentic expression. In magic, borage is thought to enhance courage. The words even rhyme. It takes courage, authentic expression, and communication to open yourself up to a new relationship and to be true to yourself in ongoing relationships.

Finally, this pudding has a sweetener, which can be used for the magical purpose of sweetening the situation. For a new relationship, the sweetener can act as an attractant for the types of people you wish to spend your time with. For an ongoing relationship, the sweetener can promote harmony and alignment with the other person.

1¼ cup nondairy milk (such as coconut milk or rice milk)
2 teaspoons fresh or dried borage flowers
1 teaspoon vanilla extract
2 teaspoons maple syrup
4 tablespoons white chia seeds

1. In a small saucepan, bring the milk to just boiling. Add the borage and remove from the heat. Allow the mixture to steep for 10 minutes.

2. Strain flowers if desired and mix in the vanilla and maple syrup. Allow the mixture to cool completely.

3. Add the chia seeds to a bowl or jar and pour the borage mixture over them. Mix thoroughly, cover, and refrigerate for at least 2 hours.

4. Eat your pudding while visualizing yourself becoming more courageous as you open yourself up to a new relationship.

CHAPTER 12

SELF-CARE FOR ABUNDANCE AND PROSPERITY

Money is called currency because it is meant to flow, like water. "Flow" is also the root of the word "affluent." Think about it this way, if your kitchen sink is clogged with food and scum, then the water can't flow freely. Similarly, if you have blockages in the path of money, it won't be able to flow to you. To feel abundant, you need to be willing to allow money to flow in and out of your presence.

You also need to be aware of what you already have. This means recognizing the moments when you feel rich and expressing gratitude. In this chapter, you will find a ritual for healing your mindset surrounding prosperity and four recipes for expressing gratitude and embracing abundance.

Unblock Your Money Mindset

For most people, money blocks and obstacles to prosperity are generally mental or emotional. To create money, you must believe that you deserve money and that having money is a good thing. Think of all the good things you can do with money.

Regardless of what your money blocks are, this spell is designed to help clear the path for more money to show up in your life. You will be invited to write down the beliefs surrounding money that you want to clear. In doing so, you are clearing your mind and making room for focused intentions, which allows for more powerful spells. Salt is used to clear, cleanse, and banish anything that does not serve you. And the fire transmutes the salt and carries your intentions into the universe.

If you have trouble thinking of your beliefs surrounding money, think of your childhood. Maybe you overheard someone say, "Money doesn't grow on trees," "We can't afford that," or some other guilt-inducing phrases about money. Maybe someone made you feel "greedy" for wanting a second slice of cake. One example of a money block is the belief that you don't deserve money. Other examples include the belief that money is bad or rich people are bad or that having nice things invites bad things, such as theft, to happen.

Do this spell as often as once a day if you need to. Stubborn beliefs didn't form overnight, and they won't always go away overnight either.

Red pen
Paper
Salt
Matches or a lighter
White candle

1. Take the red pen and sheet of paper and begin writing any money blocks that come to mind. Use as many sheets of paper as you need to write down your obstacles.

2. Sprinkle a pinch of salt onto the sheet(s) of paper. Close your eyes and visualize your blocks shrinking to the size of a grain of salt. Imagine the salt sucking the power out of the block like a vacuum.

3. Light the white candle.

4. Sprinkle a bit of salt from the paper onto the candle and say this out loud:

    This salt dissolves my limiting beliefs
    The flame transforms blocks, so I am free.
    As I will it, so it will be.

5. Sit with the candle for as long as you like, visualizing the blocks transforming and feel how this frees you. When you are ready, blow out the candle, tear up the paper(s), and go do something fun!

Prosperi-TEA

Earl Grey tea is a style of tea that is flavored with bergamot. Bergamot is a citrus fruit with an aroma that is both uplifting and calming. In magic, it is used for attracting money, opening you up to opportunities for success, and encouraging cooperation.

The practice of flavoring tea with bergamot oil dates to 1824. This was done to improve the flavor of low-quality teas. To me, this suggests a magical link to prosperity. Someone took an inferior product and adjusted it to make it better. It should be noted that some tea merchants at the time did this in a dishonest way.

It is unclear how Earl Grey tea got its name. Some suggest it is named for the British prime minister Charles Grey. Another theory is that it is named for a tea merchant named William Grey, and "Earl" was added to make the name sound classier. Even without knowing the truth, this tea blend is a billboard for abundance if you ask me.

There is no specific recipe that encompasses all Earl Grey tea. It can be made with any kind of tea leaves and flavored with oil of bergamot or dried rinds from the bergamot fruit. This recipe, also called a London Fog, is made with oat milk, Earl Grey tea blend, vanilla, and maple syrup. These ingredients combine to attract a restored mindset of peace surrounding abundance and prosperity.

EARL GREY TEA BLEND

½ cup Earl Grey tea

2 tablespoons dried cornflower

1 tablespoon lavender

1 tablespoon orange peel

LONDON FOG LATTE

½ cup water

½ cup oat milk

1 teaspoon maple syrup

1 teaspoon vanilla extract

1.   In an airtight container, mix the tea, herbs, and orange peel together. Add 1 tablespoon of tea blend to a tea strainer and place the tea strainer in a mug.

2.   In a kettle or small saucepan, bring the water to a boil. Pour the boiling water over the tea strainer. Steep for 6 to 8 minutes, then remove the tea.

3.   In a saucepan over medium-low heat, bring the oat milk to a simmer. Whisk in the maple syrup and vanilla and cook about 1 minute, or until it starts forming bubbles.

4.   Remove from the heat. Use a whisk or a frother to incorporate air into the milk. Then pour over prepared tea.

5.   Drink the tea and visualize yourself in a posh setting, surrounded by luxuries and comfort.

Rainbow Fajitas

A rainbow is something that you can experience in the physical realm. We see them when light passes through something that separates the wavelengths. For example, the sun shining through rain droplets in the sky or a light shining through a prism. It is something you can see, but it is impossible to hold in your hands. To me, this is a great metaphor for abundance.

You can experience abundance. It's the feeling of appreciation for what you have, regardless of what it is or how much you've acquired. Abundance can show up as time, money, love, inspiration, possibility, wisdom, or anything else. The point is, abundance is intangible, just like a rainbow.

The term "crossing the rainbow bridge" refers to the belief in Siberian shamanism, Greek and Norse mythology, and Vedic scripture that the rainbow is a passage between the physical and spiritual realms. Rainbows are symbolic of a connection to the source of magic and indicate good fortune is on its way.

In Irish folklore, the leprechaun is a fae creature who collects gold in pots that are hidden at the end of the rainbow. This story emerged after Vikings left Ireland, leaving behind some of their looted treasure. People began spreading stories of the mischievous leprechaun who found and rehid the Viking gold so Irish folk wouldn't find it. I know it's scientifically impossible to find the end of the rainbow because rainbows are actually perfect circles. Even so, I am filled with hope when I see a rainbow, about the potential to come across the treasure.

FAJITA SEASONING

1 tablespoon chili powder
1 teaspoon sugar
1 teaspoon ground cumin
½ teaspoon ground paprika
½ teaspoon garlic powder
½ teaspoon onion powder
½ teaspoon salt
¼ teaspoon dried oregano
¼ teaspoon cayenne pepper

FAJITA VEGGIES

Nonstick cooking spray
  (optional)
2 portobello mushroom
  caps, sliced
1 red onion, halved and sliced
1 zucchini, cut into 2-inch sticks
1 red bell pepper, sliced
1 orange bell pepper, sliced
1 yellow bell pepper, sliced
3 tablespoons extra-virgin
  olive oil

FOR SERVING

4 flour tortillas, warmed
1 avocado, sliced
1 lime, cut into wedges
2 tablespoons chopped
  fresh cilantro

½ cup fresh salsa
1 (15-ounce) can vegetarian
  refried beans, warmed
1 cup cooked rice

1. Preheat the oven to 400°F. In a small bowl, combine the seasoning ingredients. Cover a baking sheet with parchment paper or coat it with nonstick cooking spray (if using).

2. On the prepared baking sheet, arrange the vegetables in a single layer. Drizzle with the olive oil and sprinkle the seasoning blend over the top. Gently stir and toss the vegetables to evenly coat with oil and seasoning.

3. Transfer the baking sheet into the preheated oven and roast for 40 minutes, or until the vegetables wilt and brown, stirring about halfway through.

4. Remove the vegetables from the oven and serve in warmed flour tortillas, with sliced avocado, lime wedges, cilantro, salsa, vegetarian refried beans, and rice.

5. Eat your fajitas while visualizing yourself finding the leprechaun's gold at the end of a rainbow.

Avocado Toast

I knew I wanted to include a recipe for avocado toast in this book. At one point, I had it in the self-love chapter because of the concentration of heart-healthy fats and the common use of avocado in glamour spells. I also tried it out in the chapter for difficult emotions because it is easy to make when I'm having a hard time but still need to feed myself. I thought it might fit in the chapter about relationships because it can be useful for "smoothing" out arguments. I briefly fit it into the creativity chapter because it serves as a blank canvas for creative flavors.

Ultimately, it makes the most sense to include this recipe here when we're talking about abundance. For one thing, it has an abundance of magical possibilities. For another thing, the most common magical use for avocados is for abundance. The flesh is creamy and dense, which are qualities associated with abundance. The color green is associated with prosperity, wealth, and growth. Additionally, when you slice an avocado in half, the side with the pit resembles a pregnant belly: a symbol of fertility and abundance.

The pit itself corresponds with the earth element, which rules over material possessions and money. Save the pit to use in other magic spells. When fresh, it can be sliced and carved into.

I haven't even mentioned the cultural meme that the generation called "millennials" can't afford houses because we are out spending too much money on avocado toast. This magically links avocado toasts to a highly valued commodity. Admittedly, avocados can be pretty expensive, which also lends to the abundant feel of this meal.

There are countless variations when it comes to toppings for your avocado toast. This recipe is topped with sprouts, so you can sprout your feelings of abundance and be reminded to count your many blessings. You'll also add red pepper flakes, which add a small amount of spice and help speed up the blessings that are on their way.

2 sourdough bread slices
1 garlic clove
1 avocado
1 teaspoon freshly squeezed lemon juice
¼ teaspoon salt
1 cup sprouts
1 teaspoon red pepper flakes

1. Toast the bread until it is golden brown. While warm, rub the garlic clove on each toast slice.

2. Halve the avocado, remove the pit, and scoop the flesh into a bowl. Add the lemon juice and salt. Gently mash the avocado with a fork and combine the ingredients.

3. Scoop half the avocado mixture onto each slice of bread and use the fork to spread it to the edges.

4. Top with the sprouts and red pepper flakes.

5. Eat your avocado toast while visualizing your blessings sprouting and growing abundantly.

Cinnamon Sugar Cookies

The first time I made these cookies, I thought I was the richest person alive. There was nothing on earth I wanted more than to eat one, or two, or three more of these delectable treasures. Now, it has become a holiday tradition, and my dad always asks when I'll be making "the cinnamon ones" again.

Upon discovering that cinnamon is often associated with wealth and abundance, it became clear why these cookies are valued so highly in my family. Cinnamon can be described as both spicy and sweet, which is why it is an ingredient found in both savory and dessert recipes. Spicy foods amplify and expediate magic, and sweet foods attract and propagate magic. The result of the combination of the two is fast-growing wealth.

The ground cinnamon that you are most likely to find in the grocery store is cassia. It is easier to cultivate and grows in more places, therefore it is cheaper for mass distribution. Ceylon cinnamon is more expensive and harder to find but is considered "true" cinnamon. They have the same magical properties. They can also be used for culinary purposes in the same way, though cassia is spicier, and Ceylon is sweeter.

The other ingredients in these cookies are mostly there to help the cinnamon shine. The sugar sweetens the magic, the margarine holds the magic together, and the flour creates structure. On occasion, the dough is too crumbly to work with. If this happens to you, add a small amount of almond milk or water to wet the dough.

1 cup softened margarine (such as Earth Balance)
½ cup granulated sugar
½ cup firmly packed brown sugar
2 cups all-purpose flour
1½ tablespoons cinnamon
½ teaspoon baking soda

1. Preheat the oven to 325°F.

2. In a large bowl, mix the margarine and sugars vigorously until smooth and creamy.

3. In another bowl, stir the flour, cinnamon, and baking soda to combine.

4. Slowly add the dry ingredients to the wet ingredients. Stir until thoroughly incorporated.

5. Roll the dough into 1-inch balls and place on an ungreased cookie sheet, about 2 inches apart.

6. Bake for 8 to 10 minutes or until lightly browned on the edges.

7. Eat a cookie anytime you are paying bills or doing something surrounding finances to encourage a positive mindset about the flow of money.

✦ A Final Word ✦

Congratulations! You are at the end of this part of your journey as you learn about healing through self-care practices and kitchen witchcraft. As you go on to learn more from other guides and your own experiences, I hope you continue to use this book for reference and repeat the rituals, remedies, and recipes whenever you need. My goal in writing it was to open the kitchen door to you and invite you to explore my beliefs and practices.

I want you to remember that the tips and techniques I share in this book are not what make your kitchen a sacred space for healing. The way you interpret these words and implement these rituals in your life and in your home is at the heart of your magical practice. May your hearth always hold a merry fire to share warmth to all who gather around it.

Glossary

altar/shrine: A dedicated sacred space. An altar is usually an area where you work magic actively through casting spells, meditating, divining messages, etc. A shrine is an area where magic is a passive display, such as a visual representation of your magical intention, deity, or ancestor.

correspondences: Magical links between things that exist in the spiritual realm (the four elements, planets, zodiac signs, deities, ancestors, and spirits, etc.) and things that exist in the physical realm (plants, animals, rocks, color, symbols, objects, etc.).

deosil: Moving something in a clockwise direction in the Northern Hemisphere and counterclockwise in the Southern Hemisphere to increase something in your life.

grimoire: A personalized book that contains magical information about food, ingredients, timing, correspondences, tools, and other knowledge that is relevant to your kitchen witchcraft practice.

healing: A process of repairing something that has been broken, injured, or damaged, such as a body part, relationship, or connection to emotions, spirit, or creativity.

hearth: Literally, the floor of the fireplace on which a fire is made. In witchcraft, it refers to the heart of the home, where people gather together and a symbolic representation of the basis for magical power.

self-care: The practice of seeking long-term health and well-being through recognizing and honoring your needs and creating habits, rituals, and routines that benefit every area of your life.

visualization: A practice in which you use all your available senses to form a detailed mental picture of the outcome you want from conducting a ritual.

widdershins: Moving something in a counterclockwise direction in the Northern Hemisphere and clockwise in the Southern Hemisphere to decrease something in your life.

witch: Any person who decides to connect with the magical energy that flows through our universe to make changes to their circumstances through thinking, speaking, and acting with intention.

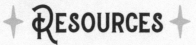

RESOURCES

Podcast

Talk Witchcraft Maggie's podcast, with co-host Erica, where witchcraft is a lifestyle and the goal is seeing magic in the mundane as you develop your personal practice.

Websites

Awesome on 20 (awesomeon20.com) A blog by Renee Rendall full of recipes that help you live your most delicious life and make every day a little bit magical and a lot more awesome.

Mumbles Academy (mumblesacademy.com) Maggie's school for witches that guides you through developing a magical mindset, equipping your witchy tool kit, and training your witchcraft skillset.

Books

***Hearth Witch's Compendium: Magical and Natural Living for Every Day* by Anna Franklin** A guide for hearth witchcraft full of recipes for food and drink, bath and beauty, cleaning, healing remedies, and spiritual wisdom.

***Kitchen Witch: Food, Folklore & Fairy Tale* by Sarah Robinson** An exploration of food, nature, magic, and transformation while following the name of the kitchen witch through time and space.

***Practical Magic for Beginners: Exercises, Rituals, and Spells for the New Mystic* by Maggie Haseman** A collection of everyday rituals and spells with instructions on a dozen entry-level practices.

REFERENCES

Bregman, Rutger, and Elizabeth Manton. *Humankind: A Hopeful History*. London, United Kingdom: Bloomsbury Publishing, 2021.

Cunningham, Scott. *Cunningham's Encyclopedia of Wicca in the Kitchen*. Woodbury, Minnesota: Llewellyn Publications, 2013.

———. *Encyclopedia of Magical Herbs*. Woodbury, Minnesota: Llewellyn, 1985.

Cunningham, Scott, and David Harrington. *The Magical Household: Spells & Rituals for the Home*. Woodbury, Minnesota: Llewellyn Publications, 2016.

Dixon-Kennedy, Mike. *Celtic Myth & Legend: An A–Z of People and Places*. London, United Kingdom: Blandford, 1997.

Forest, Danu, and Dan Goodfellow. *Magical Year: Seasonal Celebrations to Honour Nature's Ever-Turning Wheel*. London, United Kingdom: Watkins, an imprint of Watkins Media Limited, 2016.

Franklin, Anna. *The Hearth Witch's Compendium: Magical and Natural Living for Every Day*. Woodbury, Minnesota: Llewellyn Publications, 2017.

Franklin, Benjamin. *Poor Richard's Almanack*. New York: Peter Pauper Press, 1980.

Greer, John Michael. *Encyclopedia of Natural Magic*. Woodbury, Minnesota: Llewellyn, 2005.

Haseman, Maggie. *Practical Magic for Beginners: Exercises, Rituals, and Spells for the New Mystic*. New York: Rockridge Press, 2020.

Hemphill, Rosemary. *Herbs for All Seasons*. London, United Kingdom: Cassell, 1993.

Hoffman, Rachel. *Unf*ck Your Habitat: You're Better than Your Mess*. New York: St. Martin's Griffin, 2017.

Holmes, Peter. *The Energetics of Western Herbs*. Santa Rosa, California: Snow Lotus Press, 1989.

Janssen, Mary Beth. *The Book of Self-Care: Remedies for Healing Mind, Body, and Soul*. New York: Sterling Ethos, 2017.

Johnson, Cait. *Witch in the Kitchen: Magical Cooking for All Seasons*. New York: Destiny Books, 2001.

Kesten, Deborah. *Feeding the Body, Nourishing the Soul: Essentials of Eating for Physical, Emotional, and Spiritual Well-Being*. Newburyport, Massachusetts: Conari Press, 1997.

Liddon, Angela. *The Oh She Glows Cookbook*. London, United Kingdom: Penguin Michael Joseph, 2015.

Linn, Denise. *Sacred Space: Clearing and Enhancing the Energy of Your Home*. London, United Kingdom: Ebury Digital, 2010.

Lipscomb, Suzannah. *A History of Magic Witchcraft & the Occult*. London, United Kingdom: DK Publishing, 2020.

Lorde, Audre. *A Burst of Light and Other Essays*. New York: Ixia Press, 2017.

Moone, Aurora. "Herb + Plant Magickal Correspondences Archives." *Plentiful Earth*, plentifulearth.com/topics /magickal-correspondences/herb-plant-magickal-correspondences.

Patrick-Goudreau, Colleen. *Color Me Vegan: Maximize Your Nutrient Intake and Optimize Your Health by Eating Antioxidant-Rich, Fiber-Packed, Color-Intense Meals*. Beverly, Massachusetts: Fair Winds Press, 2010.

Pennick, Nigel. *Secrets of East Anglian Magic*. London, United Kingdom: Robert Hale, 1995.

Pollan, Michael. *The Botany of Desire: A Plant's-Eye View of the World*. New York: Random House, 2014.

———. *Cooked: A Natural History of Transformation*. New York: Penguin, 2014.

Raven, Gwion. *The Magick of Food: Rituals, Offerings & Why We Eat Together*. Woodbury, Minnesota: Llewellyn Worldwide, Ltd, 2020.

Raven, J. E., et al. *Plants and Plant Lore in Ancient Greece*. Oxford, United Kingdom: Leopard's Head, 2000.

Rendall, Renee. "Kitchen Magick." *Awesome on 20*, April 24, 2022, awesomeon20.com/kitchen-magick.

Rose, Carol. *Spirits, Fairies, Leprechauns, and Goblins: An Encyclopedia*. New York: W. W. Norton & Company, 2006.

Starhawk. *The Spiral Dance*. New York: Harper & Row, 1979.

Tisserand, Robert. *The Art of Aromatherapy*. London, United Kingdom: The C. W. Daniel Company Ltd, 2009.

Tresidder, Jack. *1,001 Symbols: An Illustrated Guide to Imagery and Its Meaning*. San Francisco: Chronicle Books, 2004.

Zakroff, Laura Tempest. *The Witch's Cauldron: The Craft, Lore & Magick of Ritual Vessels*. Woodbury, Minnesota: Llewellyn Worldwide, Limited, 2019.

+ INDEX +

C

Cabbage, 42, 68–69
Caffeine, 90, 126, 132
Calendula, 41, 102–103
Candles, 36, 54–55
Cardamom, 40, 78–79, 114–115
Cauldrons, 48
Cauliflower, 42
Cayenne pepper, 126–127
Celery, 42
Centering, 124–125
Chai, 114–115
Chamomile, 41, 90–91, 102–103
Cheese/vegan cheese
    substitutes, 45
Cherries, 43
Chia seeds, 45, 116–117, 144–145
Chickpeas, 45
Chile peppers, 40
Chives, 140–141
Chocolate, 40
Cilantro, 40, 128–129
Cinnamon, 40, 156–157
Cinnamon Sugar Cookies,
    156–157
Citrine, 55
Citrus fruits, 126
Clari-TEA, 66–67
Cleansing, 37, 88–89
Cleansing Vegetable Soup, 94–95
Cloves, 40
Coconut, 43
Coconut milk, 96–97
Coconut oil, 47
Coffee, 47
Colors, 36, 55
Comforting PB&J Oatmeal, 80–81

Comforting Vegan Mac-N-Yeez,
    106–107
Connected Coconut Cream, 96–97
Connected to Spirit Salad, 92–93
Cookware, 47–49
Coriander, 40, 128–129
Corn, 44, 128–129
Cottage witches, 4
Courageous Borage Chia
    Pudding, 144–145
Creativi-TEA, 126–127
Creativity. See Energy and
    creativity, self-care for
Creole seasoning, 130–131
"Crossing the rainbow bridge," 152
Crystals, 36, 55–56
Cucumbers, 42
Cumin, 40
Cups, elemental alignment of, 49

D

Divination, 92
Doctrine of signatures, 68

E

Earl Grey tea, 150–151
Earth element, 50
Echinacea, 41, 138–139
Eggs/vegan egg substitutes, 45
Elderberries, 43, 138–139
Elements, 36, 50
Emotional Expression West
    African Peanut Stew, 108–109
Emotions, self-care for difficult
    about, 19–20, 99
    Comforting Vegan Mac-N-Yeez,
        106–107

Acknowledgments

In many ways, this book is a memorial for my grandmother. I consulted with her about cooking while she was alive, and she continues to be a consultant from the spirit realm since she passed through in February 2020. I would like to acknowledge her life with these words. I also want to thank my husband, Dana, for taste testing these recipes, being understanding of the extra hours at work, and taking care of me throughout the process. Thank you to my mother for teaching me to cook and passing on the love of housekeeping. Thank you to my father for showing me what it means to be spiritual and compassionate and always giving sage advice. I also want to express gratitude to my in-laws for taking such good care of me while I was putting together the final draft. To all my friends and family members who cheered me on, especially my sister, Erica, thank you for your faith in me. Finally, a big thanks to the publishing team, who took my words and made a beautiful book.

About the Author

Maggie Haseman has been a student and practitioner of folk witchcraft and natural magic since 2013. As the HeadWITCHstress of Mumbles Academy, she creates courses, podcasts, articles, books, and videos about witchcraft, personal development, and spirituality. Her goal is to spread magic, build community, and cultivate kindness among witches around the world. She is a game-loving, tea-drinking vegan with ADHD. She's a feminist, an environmentalist, and a social justice activist. Maggie lives in St. Petersburg, Florida, with her husband, Dana, and their two cats, Luna and Nox. For more information about Maggie and her teaching, visit MumblesAndThings.com.